BEGINNERS, PLEASE!

with pitman 2000

Doreen Sharp

FRSA, FSCT, FFT(Com)
Senior Lecturer in Charge Secretarial Studies
Department of Business and Social Sciences
Bromley College of Technology

PITMAN

PITMAN PUBLISHING LIMITED
39 Parker Street, London WC2B 5PB

Associated Companies
Copp Clark Ltd, Toronto · Pitman Publishing Corporation/Fearon
Publishers Inc, Belmont, California · Pitman Publishing Co. SA (Pty) Ltd,
Johannesburg · Pitman Publishing New Zealand Ltd, Wellington
Pitman Publishing Pty Ltd, Melbourne

Text set in 10/11 pt IBM Journal,
printed by photolithography and bound in Great Britain
at The Pitman Press, Bath

ISBN 0 273 00871 4

(2012: 26)

Publisher's Preface

Beginners, Please! with Pitman 2000 enables the student of *Pitman 2000 First Course* to revise the shorthand theory at regular intervals. The first Assignments are intended for use when Unit 10 of *First Course* has been completed and, subsequently, after Units 14, 17 and 21. In this way, the shorthand learning is integrated with speed development and transcription training.

The Assignments are designed to give practice in the basic points of typewriting technique and English usage; they give the student an opportunity to produce mailable transcripts at each stage of the shorthand theory learning. The answers to the Background Information Exercises are printed at the back of the book.

This text is based on the author's successful articles in Pitman *2000* magazine.

Contents

Units 1-10

Short Form and Phrase Drill

date the .... , today .... , several .... , days ago .... , our .... , in .... ,

they are .... , with the .... , it is .... , that the .... , largest .... , for .... , I have .... ,

without delay ....

High Frequency Words

them .... , market .... , most ....

Theory — Circle 's', loop 'st', stroke 's'

Circle 's', loop 'st' inside curves:

Soames	....	Thomas	....	sale	....	sent	....
message	....	vast	....	science	....	maths	....
less	....	slow	....	sales	....		

Circle 's', loop 'st' anti-clockwise to straight strokes:

| texts | .... | Telex | .... | latest | .... | tapes | .... |
| stated | .... | spare | .... | depots | .... | | |

Circle 's' outside the angle formed by two straight strokes:

| cassettes | .... | despatch | .... |

Stroke 's' when 's' is the only consonant in a word:

| us | .... | so | .... |

Stroke 's' when a vowel is sounded before 's' at the beginning of a word:

| asked | .... | estates | .... |

Reading — Memo

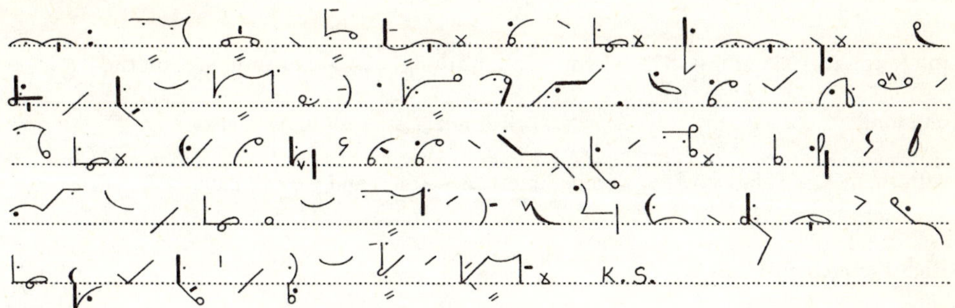

Dictation

Memo: Kenneth Soames to Thomas Dunmow. Sale of texts. Date[10] the memo today. Several days ago our depot in Atlanta[20] sent us a Telex message regarding the vast sales of[30] our latest science and maths texts. They are less delighted[40] with the slow sales of back-up tapes and cassettes.[50] It is stated that the largest market for our texts[60] is in Canada and so I have asked them to[70] despatch most of the spare texts without delay to our[80] depots on our estates in Ottawa and Toronto. K.S.[90]

(90 words)

Typing Drill

(*a*) Our depot sent us a Telex message.   7

(*b*) The largest market for our texts is in Canada.   9

(*c*) I have asked them to despatch most of the spare texts.   11

Background Information Exercise — Cities and Towns

Make two columns and head one CANADA and the other USA. Check in an atlas, if necessary, and list the following cities and towns in alphabetical order under the correct heading:

Detroit, Calgary, Minnesota, Edmonton, Montreal, Milwaukee, Quebec, Philadelphia, Chicago, Winnipeg.

Production — Memorandum

Use A5 paper turned sideways. Type in blocked style. Copy this heading first:

MEMORANDUM

FROM: TO:

SUBJECT: DATE:

Units 1-10

Short Form and Phrase Drill

too long .... , at my .... , I am .... , nothing .... , to stay .... , on the .... ,

on Monday .... , my way .... , I shall not .... , to do .... , also .... ,

with them .... , but you .... , immediately .... , and we will have ....

High Frequency Words

because .... , next .... , month .... , nice .... , much ....

Theory — Dot 'ing'

A dot at the end of an outline represents the suffix 'ing':

saving ....   taking ....   going ....   boating ....

sunning ....   setting ....   making ....   writing ....

staying ....

Reading — Personal Letter

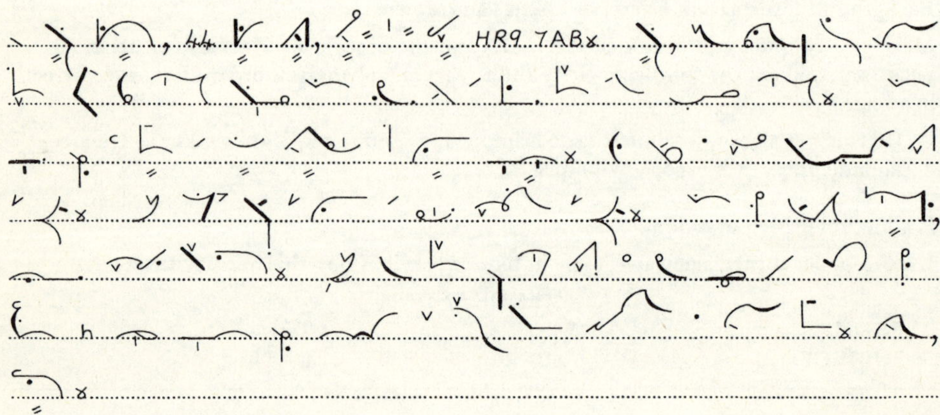

Dictation

To Beth Taylor, 44 Dale Road, Ross-on-Wye[10] HR9 7AB. Beth, I have slaved[20] far too long at my job this month because I[30] am saving up and taking time off next month. I[40] am going to stay with Tom and Anne Robson at[50] Lake Como. They possess a nice bungalow right on the[60] shore. I shall enjoy boating on the lake and sunning[70] myself on the shore. I am setting forth on Monday,[80] making my way by car. I shall not have time[90] to do much writing as several guests are also staying[100] with them but you must come to stay immediately I[110] arrive back and we will have a long talk. Love,[120] Claire.

(121 words)

Typing Drill

(a)	They possess a nice bungalow.	6
(b)	I shall enjoy boating on the lake.	7
(c)	I shall not have time to do much writing.	8
(d)	I am setting forth on Monday, making my way by car.	10

Background Information Exercise — Lakes

Make a list, in alphabetical order, of the following European lakes. Beside each, type the name of the country in which the lake is situated. Check in an atlas if necessary:

Como, Balaton, Windermere, Garda, Bala, Siljan, Brienz, Nantua, Gruyères.

Production — Personal Letter

Use A5 paper. Put your own home address at the top right-hand corner and put today's date. Address the letter to Miss Beth Taylor. Block the addresses but use the indented style for the text of the letter.

Units 1-10

Short Form and Phrase Drill

of this note ...., is to........, of my............, with ...., at his ...., this ....,

first-class ...., which ...., had ...., that ...., large............, would ...., almost ....,

and I know ....

High Frequency Words

object ...., tell ...., made ...., end ....

Theory — 'Ses' circle

The sound of Ses, Sez, Zes or Zez is represented by a large circle written at the end of an outline:

success   ....   replaces   ....   access   ....   places   ....

excess   ....

Reading — Memo

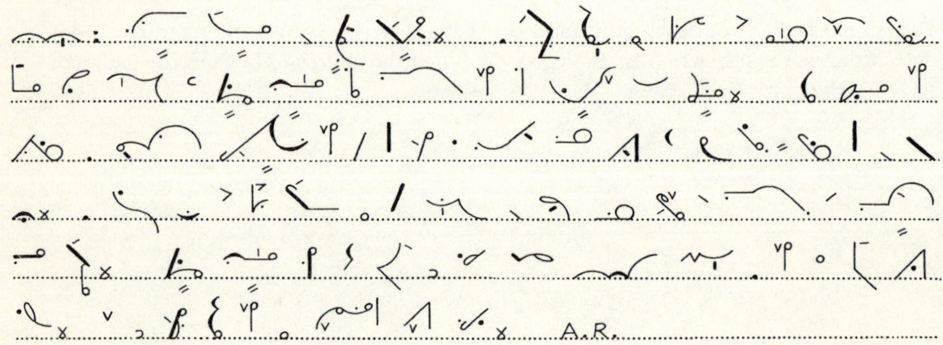

Assignment 3

Dictation

Memo: Alec Fox to Joseph Burrows. The object of this[10] note is to tell you of the success of my[20] pleasant talks last month with James Maddox at his camp[30] site at Fairlight in Sussex. This first-class site replaces[40] the smaller Worthing site which had such a narrow access[50] road that several passing-places had to be made. The[60] far end of the toilet block is large enough to[70] store excess supplies of camping and Calor gas bottles. James[80] Maddox said that the shop would start almost immediately and[90] I know the site has top rate staff. I would[100] suggest that this site is licensed right away. A.R.[110]

(110 words)

Typing Drill

(*a*)	I know the site has top rate staff.	7
(*b*)	Several passing-places had to be made.	8
(*c*)	I would suggest that this site is licensed right away.	11
(*d*)	James Maddox said that the shop would start almost immediately.	13

Background Information Exercise — Antonyms

By adding a prefix to some words you can form words of opposite meaning. These are known as *antonyms*. Type the following words and alongside each word type its antonym:

appear, pleasant, licensed, pure, attentive, approve, legitimate, relevant, trust.

Production — Memorandum

Use A5 paper turned sideways. Type in blocked style. Date it today. The subject heading is Fairlight Camp Site.

Units 1-10

Short Form and Phrase Drill

let you know............, I have ...., which you............, days ago ....,

have not yet ...., are you............, for the first time............, and this has ....,

at this............, although ...., I know that ...., will be ...., at some ....,

I know that we have ...., thinking............, which should be ...., I will ....,

on you............, tomorrow............

High Frequency Words

short............, report............, work............, those............, call............

Theory — Past-tense sounds 't' and 'd'

Past tenses are shown by writing a disjoined stroke 't' or 'd' (according to whichever is sounded) close to the root outline:

posted	talked	asked	added
caused	unexpected	budgeted	marked
ended	muddled	developed	supported

Reading — Memo

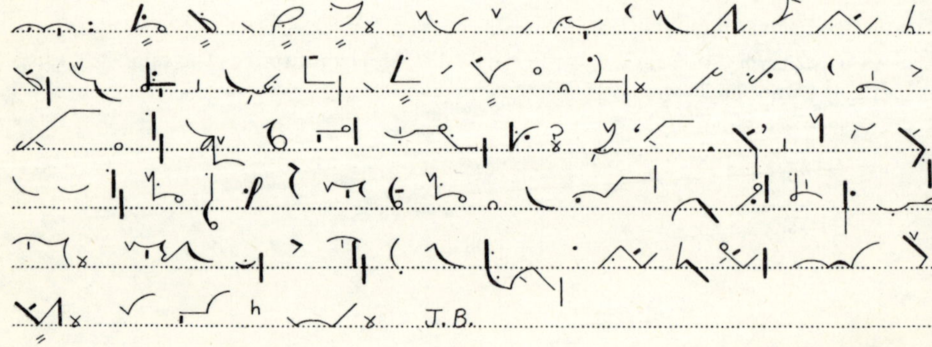

Assignment 4

Dictation

Memo: James Best to Lester Nash. I felt I should[10] let you know that I have read the short report[20] which you posted five days ago but have not yet[30] talked to Jack and Paul as you asked. Are you[40] aware that some of the work is added for the[50] first time and this has caused unexpected delay? I shall[60] not 'rock the boat' but I had not budgeted for[70] any added items at this stage although I know that[80] those items you have marked will be raised at some[90] date next month. I know that we have ended all[100] the muddled thinking and have developed a report which should[110] be supported immediately by the Board. I will call on[120] you tomorrow. J.B.

(124 words)

Typing Drill

(a)	I have read the short report which you posted.	9
(b)	Some of the work is added for the first time.	9
(c)	I shall not 'rock the boat' but I had not budgeted for any added items.	15

Background Information Exercise — Metaphorical Expressions

Here are six metaphorical expressions. Can you say very briefly what they mean? Type your answers:

(i) to rock the boat;
(ii) to swim against the tide;
(iii) to call a spade a spade;
(iv) to turn a blind eye;
(v) to hold out an olive branch;
(vi) to sail under false colours.

Production — Memorandum

Use A5 paper turned sideways. Type in blocked style and use today's date.

Units 1-10

Short Form and Phrase Drill

& Sons ...., have had ...., in your ...., for some ...., I must ....,

have this ...., without ...., ask you ...., should be glad ....,

immediately ...., unable to ...., all the ...., by this ...., I shall ....,

with you ...., thinking ...., yours ....

High Frequency Words

come ...., word ...., third ....

Theory — Upward and Downward 'r'

Upwards: At the end of an outline when 'r' is followed by a sounded vowel:

        Murray ....   Burrows ....

        When 'r' begins a word:

        road ....   repair ....   writing ....

        In the middle of an outline:

        Dorset ....   park ....   Dorchester ....   workshop ....

        fortnight's ....

Downwards: When followed by circle 's':

        Messrs ....   sirs ....

        Before 'm':

        Ramsay ....

        When the sound of 'r' ends a word:

        Taylor ....

Reading – Letter

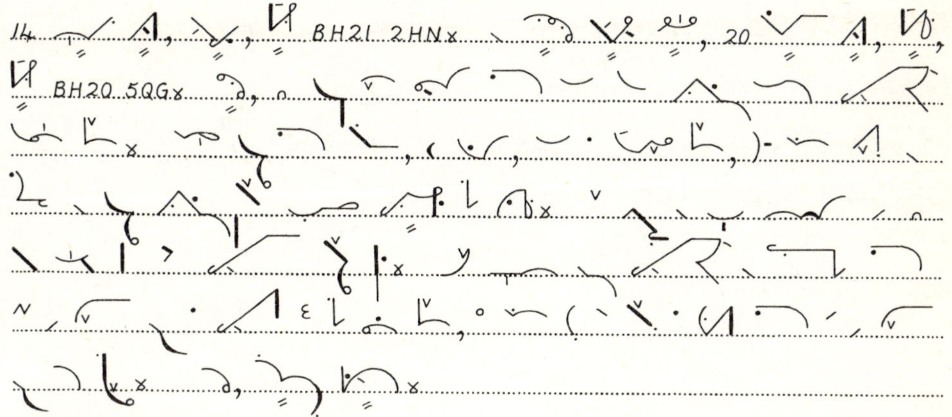

Dictation

14 Murray Road, Upway, Dorset
BH21 2[10]HN. To Messrs. Burrows & Sons,
20 Park Road,[20] Dorchester, Dorset
BH20 5QG. Sirs,[30] You have had my small
car in for repair in[40] your workshop for
some time. I must have this car[50] back,
without fail, in a fortnight's time, so I am[60]
writing to ask you to have this repaired by
next[70] Wednesday at the latest. I should
be glad to know[80] immediately should
you be unable to do all the work[90] by this
date. I shall come to your workshop to[100]
collect the car and I should like to have a[110]
word with you at the same time, as I am[120]
thinking of buying a third car and should
like to[130] have your advice. Yours,
Ramsay Taylor.

(136 words)

Typing Drill

(a) You have had my small car in for repair.   8
(b) I shall come to your workshop to collect the car.   10

Background Information Exercise – County Names in England and Wales

In alphabetical order and in two columns, type the following counties under the headings
of England and Wales:

Gwent, Avon, West Yorkshire, Gwynedd, Dyfed, Humberside, Mid Glamorgan,
Cleveland, Powys, Clwyd, Cumbria, North Yorkshire.

Production – Letter

Use A5 paper and put today's date. Use the fully-blocked style.

Units 1-10

Short Form and Phrase Drill

5th May ...., our ...., manufacturers ...., have ...., I have just ....,

I will be ...., to take ...., on the ...., we shall go ...., to some ....,

who will be ...., in the ...., we shall be ...., on Saturday ....,

to come ...., hours ....

High Frequency Words

them ...., call ...., sent ...., off ...., next ...., coming ....

Theory — Upward and Downward 'r'

Upward 'r':

Charles ....   Russell ....   Derek ....   Rhodes ....

Carraway ....   Sarah ....   Bird ....   part ....

Antwerp ....

Downward 'r':

Rome ....   air ....   Norma ....   firms ....

airport ....   car ....

Reading — Memo

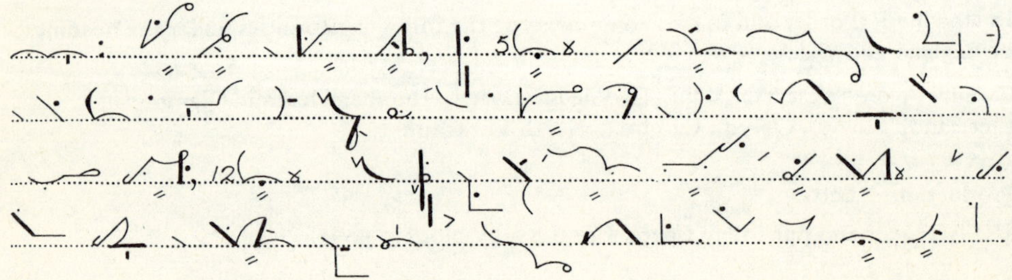

Dictation

Memo: Charles Russell to Derek Rhodes, dated 5th May. Our[10] Rome manufacturers have asked us to pay them a call[20] so I have just sent off a Telex message to[30] say that I will be going by air next Wednesday,[40] 12th May. I have decided to take both Norma Carraway[50] and Sarah Bird. On the way back we shall go[60] to Belgium to talk to some of the firms who[70] will be taking part in the May Show at Antwerp.[80] We shall be coming back on Saturday, 15th May and[90] I should like you to come to the airport to[100] fetch us in the car at 1100 hours. C.R.[110]

(111 words)

Typing Drill

(*a*)	On the way back we shall go to Belgium.	8
(*b*)	I should like you to come to the airport.	8
(*c*)	I have decided to take both Norma and Sarah.	9
(*d*)	Our Rome manufacturers have asked us to pay them a call.	12

Background Information Exercise — Memorandum quiz

  (i)   What is a memorandum?
 (ii) How does it differ from a letter?
(iii) Is it signed by the sender?
(iv) Should a memo be typed in blocked or indented form?

Production — Memorandum

Use A5 paper turned sideways. Put a subject heading 'Visit to Rome' and type in indented style.

Units 1-10

Short Form and Phrase Drill

I am ...., that ...., our ...., to do the ...., so much ...., I shall be ....,

in fact ...., I shall have ...., I think you ...., who are .... , also ....,

and we think the ...., but you will have ...., yourself ...., that you ....,

could ...., to make the ...., we think you will ....

High Frequency Words

tell ...., going ...., because ....

Theory — Half-length strokes

In words of ONE syllable:

A thin stroke may be halved to indicate a following 't':

Knight's .... Pat .... Kate .... acting ....

part .... Tate .... thought ....

A thick stroke may be halved to indicate a following 'd':

Dodd .... Budd ....

In words of TWO or more syllables:

Strokes may be halved to indicate a following 't' or 'd':

Matlock .... delighted .... support .... result ....

Reading — Personal Letter

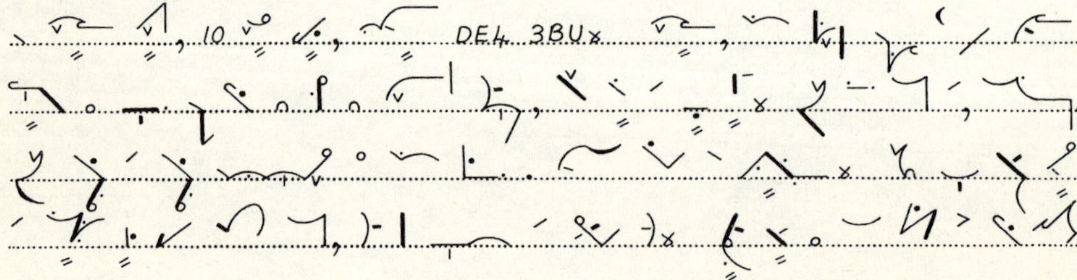

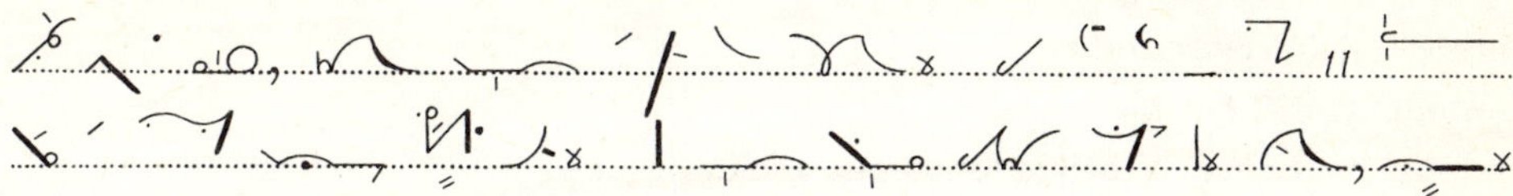

Dictation

To Michael Wright, 10 Knight's Way, Matlock DE4[10] 3BU. Michael, I am delighted to tell you[20] that our local Club is going to do the play[30] you said you liked so much, by Pat and Kate[40] Dodd. I shall be acting in it and, in fact,[50] I shall have pages and pages to memorise as I[60] am taking the long part of Rebecca. I think you[70] know both Ross and Angela Tate who are also in[80] it, so do come and support us. Joseph Budd is[90] in charge of the play and we think the result[100] should be a success, but you will have to come[110] and judge for yourself. We thought that you could catch[120] the eleven o'clock bus and manage to make the Saturday[130] show. Do come because we think you will enjoy it.[140] Love, Meg.

(142 words)

Typing Drill

(*a*)	Our local Club is going to do the play.	8
(*b*)	I shall have pages and pages to memorise.	8
(*c*)	I think you know both Ross and Angela Tate.	9

Background Information Exercise — Using the apostrophe

Type the following sentences, adding an apostrophe wherever one is needed:

(i)   The shop sells both mens and womens clothing.

(ii)   The childs dog was wagging its tail.

(iii)   I spoke to the Warden of the childrens home.

(iv)   I cant really afford the time to go to the show but will make an effort as youre playing such an important part.

(v)   Is the pen hers or yours?

Production — Letter

Use A5 paper. Address it from 29 Lark's Drive, Belper DE5 1GE. Put today's date. Block the addresses but indent the text of the letter.

Units 1-10

Theory — Half-length strokes

In words of ONE syllable:

A thin stroke may be halved to indicate a following 't':

Kate   coats   nut   tart

A thick stroke may be halved to indicate a following 'd':

Jade

In words of TWO or more syllables:

Strokes may be halved to indicate a following 't' or 'd':

Janet   Watson   Jackets   Cottage

omelette   cutlets   vegetables   potatoes

carrots   chocolate   assorted

Reading — Menu

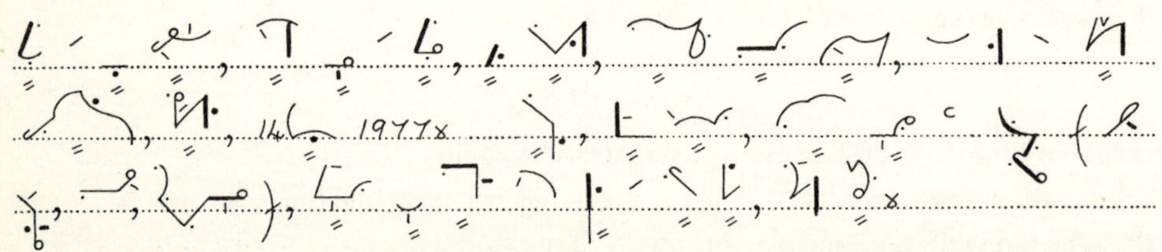

Dictation

> Janet & Kate Watson
> Model Coats and Jackets
> Jade Parade
> Manchester
> Gala Lunch
> In aid of Child Welfare
> Saturday, 14th May 1977

Pâté
Duck Omelette
Lamb Cutlets with Vegetables
(roast potatoes, carrots, asparagus)
Chocolate Nut Gâteau
or
Date and Apple Tart
Assorted Ices

Typing Drill and Background Information Exercise — Spacing of Letters and Words

Drill the following so that you practise the proper spacing of letters and words:

(*a*)   Using spaced capitals — *one* space between letters and *three* spaces between words:

```
J A N E T   &   K A T E   W A T S O N
```

(*b*)   Using capitals — *one* or *two* spaces between words:

```
MODEL COATS AND JACKETS

MODEL   COATS   AND   JACKETS
```

(*c*)   Using lower case letters — *one* space between words:

```
Date and Apple Tart
```

Production — Menu

Use A5 paper. Display the menu attractively and centre each item. Put 'Janet & Kate Watson' in spaced capitals, 'Model Coats and Jackets' and 'Gala Lunch' in capitals. Add a simple decorative framework. After typing, insert the accents (circumflex ˆ and acute ´) in ink, over the words 'Pâté' and 'Gâteau'.

Units 1-10

Short Form and Phrase Drill

to go ......, on the ......, on Saturday ......, it was ......, it has ......, something ......,

with the ......, first-class ......, I got ......, at first ......, we were ......, large ......,

ourselves ......, would you ......, should be ......, to have you ......

High Frequency Words

cold ......, started ......, called ......, gold ......, though ......

Theory — 'L' hook to straight strokes

A small hook at the beginning of a straight downstroke, 'k' and 'g', written on the same side as the circle 's', adds the sound of 'l':

Clara ......   Blake ......   Cloisters ......   Gloucester ......

Claud ......   Clem ......   close ......   club ......

Cloth ......   glided ......   Glenda ......

The hook 'l' may also be used in the middle of an outline:

Uncle ......   local ......   Naples ......   muddle ......

Reading — Personal Letter

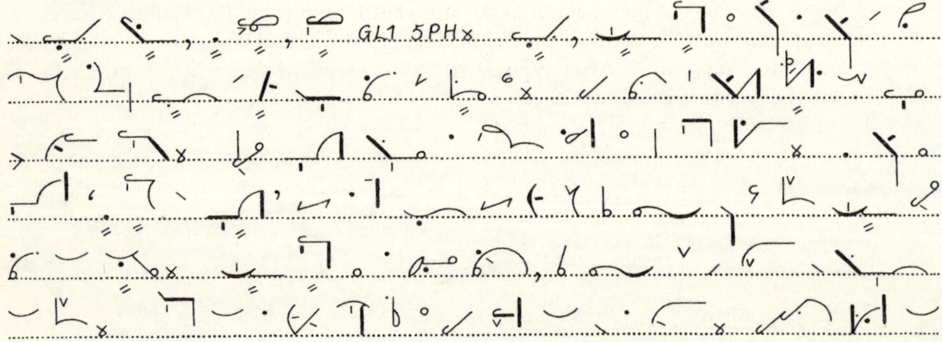

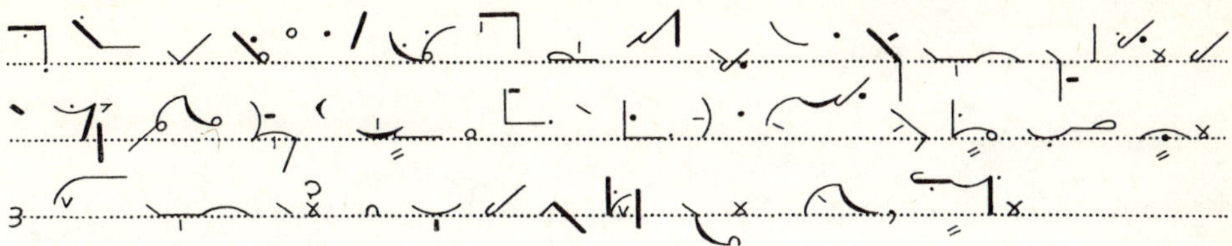

Dictation

To Clara Blake, The Cloisters, Gloucester GL1 5[10]PH. Clara, Uncle Claud has bought a boat and[20] last month asked Clem and Joe to go sailing on[30] the Thames with us. We slept on board on Saturday[40] night close to the local club. It was cold because[50] a storm started as it got dark. The boat is[60] called 'The Cloth of Gold' — an odd name — though I[70] think it has something to do with the time Uncle[80] was sailing in Naples. Uncle Claud is a first-class[90] sailor, which is something I should like to become in[100] time. I got in a thorough muddle at first as[110] we glided in to a lock. We were delayed in[120] getting back to our base as a large vessel got[130] stuck and we had to wait for a boat to[140] come to tow it away. We all enjoyed ourselves so[150] much that Uncle is talking of taking us a long[160] way up the Thames next May. Would you like to[170] come too? You know we should be delighted to have[180] you. Love, Glenda.

(183 words)

Typing Drill

(a)	Uncle Claud has bought a boat.	6
(b)	We slept on board on Saturday night.	8
(c)	We were delayed in getting back to our base.	9
(d)	Uncle is talking of taking us a long way up the Thames next May.	13

Background Information Exercise — 'I' and 'me'

Type the following sentences and put in 'I' or 'me' as necessary:

(i)   Would you like to come with Claud and . . . ?
(ii)   You and . . . will sail the boat.
(iii) Who is responsible for the damage? . . . !
(iv) The work to be undertaken by you and . . . must be finished by the end of the week.

Production — Personal Letter

Use A5 paper. Put your own home address at the top right-hand corner. Date the letter for some time in March. Send it to Miss Clara Blake at the address given. Use open punctuation and the fully-blocked style.

Units 1-10

Short Form and Phrase Drill

we have just ...., had ...., or so..........., it was ...., of our ...., of last ....,

right away ...., and we must ...., any delay ...., exchange the ....,

in time ...., first ...., to go ...., with you ...., I think we could ....,

first thing ...., tomorrow ....

High Frequency Words

call ...., respect..........., despatched..........., going ...., care..........., customer ....,

model ...., young ....

Theory — Diphthongs 'I' and 'OI'

Diphthong 'I':

Michael	....	Styles	....	Ryde	....	Isle	....
Wight	....	supply	....	time	....	like	....
Rice	....	by	....				

Diphthong 'OI':

| Doyle | .... | Roy | .... | avoid | .... | boy | .... |
| Mulloy | .... | | | | | | |

Reading — Memo

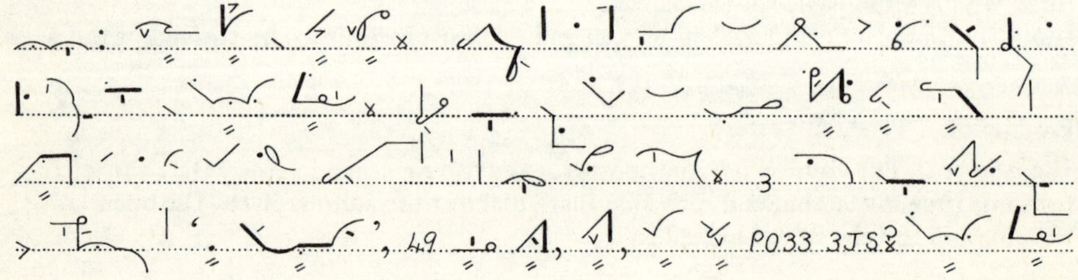

24

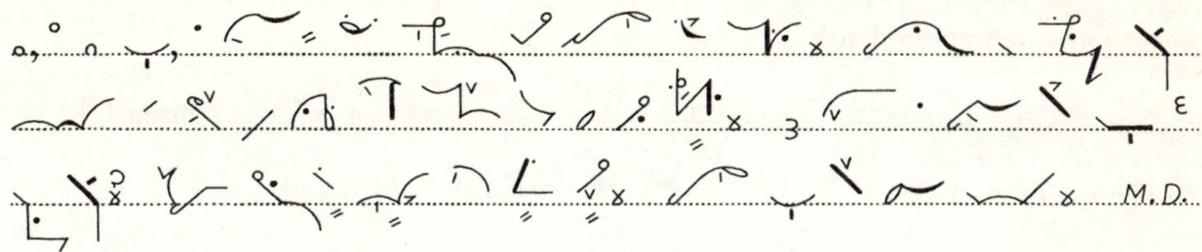

Dictation

Memo: Michael Doyle to Roy Styles. We have just had[10] an odd call in respect of the sailing boat despatched[20] a day or so ago to Pamela Jackson. It was[30] going to take part in next Saturday's Yacht Club Regatta[40] and a lot of our staff worked on it most[50] of last month. Would you care to go right away[60] to talk to the customer at 'The Bungalow', 49[70] Oaks Road, Ryde, Isle of Wight PO33[80] 3JS? Pamela Jackson is, as you know, a[90] long-standing customer of ours and we must avoid any[100] delay. We may have to exchange the boat immediately and[110] supply our latest model in time for the first race[120] on Saturday. Would you like a young boy to go[130] with you to take the boat? I think we could[140] spare Pat Mulloy or Jack Rice. We must know by[150] first thing tomorrow. M.D.

(155 words)

Typing Drill

(a) We have just had an odd call.	6
(b) We must know by first thing tomorrow.	7
(c) We may have to exchange the boat immediately.	9
(d) A lot of our staff worked on it most of last month.	10

Background Information Exercise — Spelling — 'ie' and 'ei'

Type one copy of the following which may help you with the spelling of words containing 'ie' and 'ei':

(i) Use 'ie' when it is sounded as 'ee', except after the letter 'c',
e.g. brief, relief, believe, achieve. (Exceptions: seize, weird.)

(ii) Use 'ei' when it is sounded as 'ee', after 'c',
e.g. receive, perceive, conceive, conceit.

(iii) Use 'ei' when it is sounded in any other way than 'ee',
e.g. either, feign, eight, height.

Production — Memorandum

Use A5 paper turned sideways. Type in blocked style and use today's date. Mark it URGENT in the top left-hand corner.

Units 1-10

Short Form and Phrase Drill

to take the ...., largest ...., months' time ...., and I have ...., on the ....,

all the ...., in charge ...., do you ...., think that ...., in any way ....,

would you ...., I thought ...., should be glad ...., several ...., also ....

High Frequency Words

short ...., word ...., ask ....

Theory — Loops 'st' and 'ster'

Loop 'st':

Stock .... Stella .... West .... rest ....

stores .... Stockport .... Best ....

Loop 'ster':

Chester .... Leicester .... Manchester .... Doncaster ....

Reading — Memo

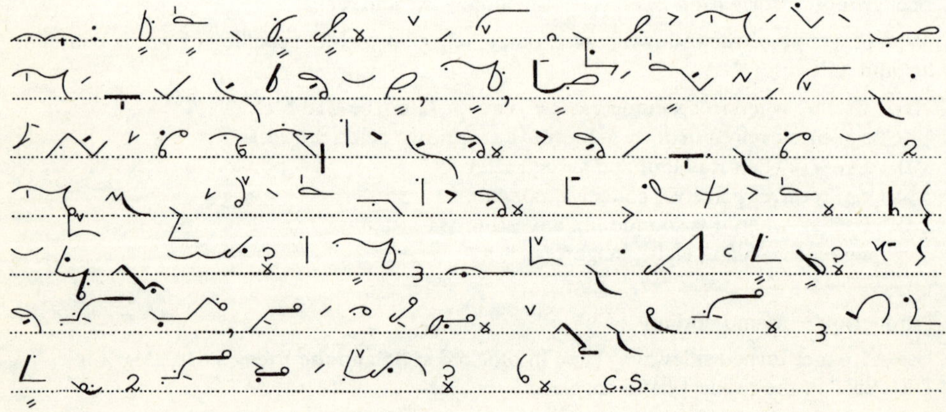

Dictation

Memo: Chester Stock to Stella West. I should like you[10] to take the rest of the month and part of[20] next month and go to our four largest stores in[30] Leicester, Manchester, Doncaster and Stockport and I should like to[40] have a short report on the sales methods employed at[50] all four stores. All the stores are going to have[60] sales in two months' time and I have to check[70] on the size of stock kept at all the stores.[80] Talk to the staff in charge of the stock. Do[90] you think that any changes should be made in any[100] way? At Manchester would you make time to have a[110] word with Jack Best? I thought that the store catalogue[120] of carpets, rugs and mats was first-class. I should[130] be glad to have several catalogues. Would you also ask[140] Jack to send two catalogues of glass- and china-ware?[150] Thanks. C.S.

(153 words)

Typing Drill

(*a*) I should be glad to have several catalogues.   9

(*b*) I should like you to go to our four largest stores.   10

(*c*) All the stores are going to have sales in two months' time. 12

Background Information Exercise — Using the apostrophe

Type a copy of this extract from *Fowler's Modern English Usage*:

It was formerly customary when a word ended in -s to write its possessive with an apostrophe, e.g. Mars' Hill, Venus' Bath.

In verse and in reverential contexts this custom is retained, e.g. Achilles', Jesus'.

Elsewhere we now usually add the 's' and the syllable, e.g. St. James's Street, Pythagoras's doctrines.

Years and weeks may be treated as possessives and given an apostrophe or as adjectival nouns without one. The former conforms to what is used in the singular, e.g. in a month's time, in two months' time, a year's imprisonment, two years' imprisonment.

Production — Memorandum

Use A5 paper turned sideways. Type in blocked form. Use a date towards the end of January.

Units 1-10

Short Form and Phrase Drill

your .... , yesterday .... , and I felt .... , that you .... , several times .... ,

so that you may .... , and I will .... , ought .... , without .... , hours .... ,

immediate .... , thing .... , will not be .... , who will .... , it should be .... ,

who is .... , unable to ....

High Frequency Words

most .... , chair .... , child ....

Theory — Strokes 'm' and 'n' halved and thickened

Strokes 'm' and 'n' are halved and thickened to add the following sound of 'd':

Sandgate ....   Wallend ....   Maud ....   End ....

Medway ....   stand ....   Ned ....

Reading — Personal letter

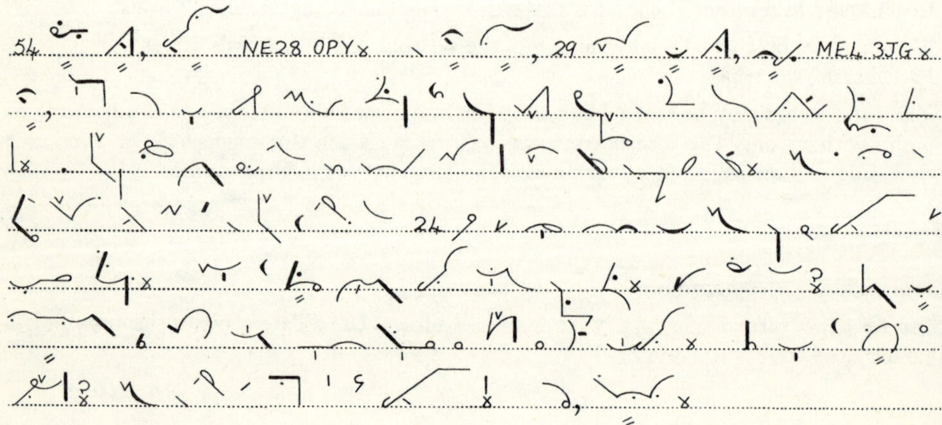

Dictation

54 Sandgate Road, Wallend NE28 0[10]PY. To Maud Lang, 29 Mile End Road,[20] Medway ME4 3JG. Maud, I got[30] your note yesterday and I felt ashamed that you have[40] had to write several times to ask for your report[50] so that you may check it. The typed masters will[60] be sent off to you tomorrow and I will do[70] my best to catch the first post. I have a[80] mass of jobs piling up and I ought to type[90] without stopping for 24 hours but the most immediate[100] thing I have to do is to work on the[110] next agenda. I know that James will not be well[120] enough to take the chair. Who will stand in? It[130] should be Ned McNab who is also unable to come[140] because his child is so unwell. Do you know that[150] Elsa has resigned? I have to stop and get on[160] with the work! Yours, Pamela.

(165 words)

Typing Drill

(*a*)	I got your note yesterday.	5
(*b*)	Do you know that Elsa has resigned?	7
(*c*)	I know that James will not be well enough.	8
(*d*)	The typed masters will be sent off to you tomorrow.	10

Background Information Exercise — Meetings

Type the following list of terms used in connection with meetings and type the meaning beside each:

(i)   agenda;
(ii) ad hoc committee;
(iii) motion;
(iv) elected member;
(v)   status quo.

Production — Personal letter

Use A5 paper, with open punctuation and fully-blocked style. Put today's date and address the letter to Mrs Maud Lang.

Units 1-10

High Frequency Words

damaged ...., much ...., rail ...., going ...., tomorrow ...., send ....,
regards ....

Theory — Revision of short forms and phrases

that	....	I shall be	....	unable to	....	to lunch	....
with you	....	on Sunday	....	I have	....	to go	....
immediately	....	as	....	who has	....	had	....
has	....	his	....	and is not	....	able to	....
do	....	anything	....	but	....	in	....
for	....	several days	....	I think	....	I shall have	....
tomorrow	....	and I have said	....	could	....	I will	....
to let you know	....	to you	....				

Reading — Personal letter

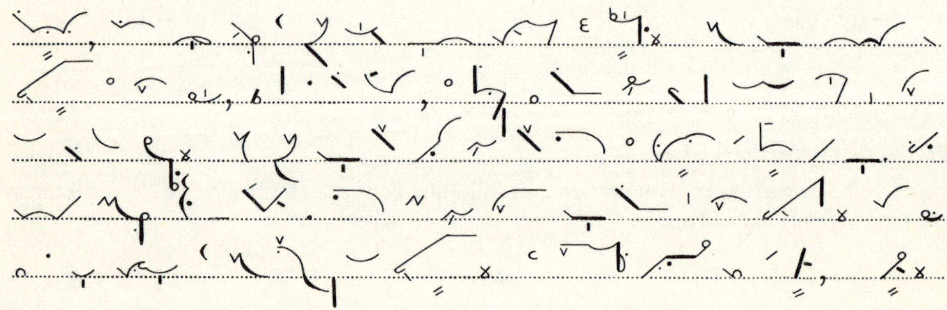

Dictation

Pamela, I am most upset that I shall be unable[10] to come to lunch with you on Sunday. I have[20] to go immediately to York as my son, who has[30] had a bad fall, has damaged his back and is[40] not able to do anything much but lie in bed[50] for several days. I think I shall have to go[60] by rail and not by car as Thelma and Tom[70] are going away tomorrow and I have said that they[80] could borrow the car and I should not like to[90] go back on my word. I will send you a[100] note to let you know that I have arrived in[110] York. With kindest regards to you and Joe, Rose.

(119 words)

Typing Drill

(a)	I shall be unable to come to lunch.	7
(b)	I think I shall have to go by rail.	7
(c)	Thelma and Tom are going away tomorrow.	8
(d)	I should not like to go back on my word.	8

Background Information Exercise — Pairs of words

Using your dictionary, look up the meanings of the following pairs of words. When you are sure that you know the difference between the words, type sentences to show their correct use:

immediately	instantaneously	welcome	acceptable
finished	finalised	external	exterior

Production — Personal letter

Use A5 paper. Put your own address in the top right-hand corner and date the letter with today's date.

Units 1-10

High Frequency Words

dated ________ , us ________ , report ________ , typed ________ , standard ________ , started ________ ,

customers ________ , most ________

Theory — Revision of phrases and intersections

27th May	days ago	yellow form	would have
as fast as	and we were	for some	so that we could
to them	it was not	for it	are unable to
I know that	this is	of us	and I am
I know	should be glad		

Reading — Memo

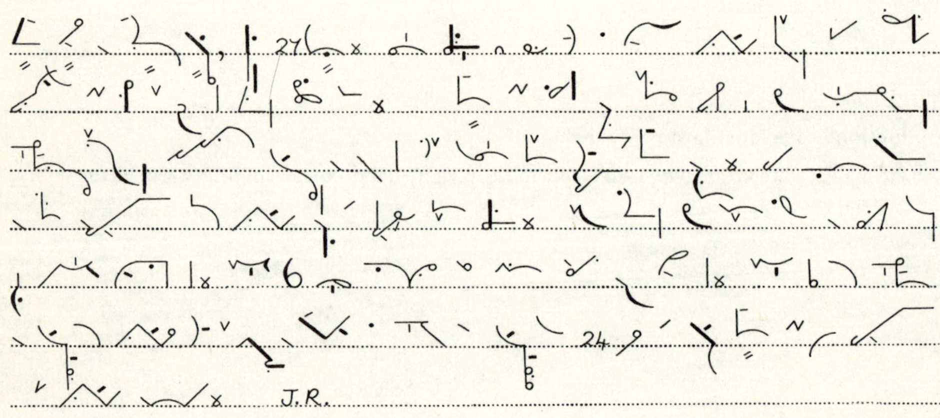

Dictation

Jock Ross to Oscar Bates, dated 27th May. Some[10] days ago you sent us a long report typed on[20] our standard yellow form and I said I would have[30] it checked as fast as I could. Tom and I[40] started to check the items yesterday but several unexpected customers[50] arrived and we were forced to put it aside for[60] some time so that we could talk to them. We[70] came back to attempt to work on your report today[80] and it was not on my desk. I have asked[90] several of my staff to search for it but they[100] are unable to locate it. I know that this is[110] most careless of us and I am sorry to have[120] lost it. I know it is your custom to photostat[130] your reports so I should be glad to borrow a[140] couple of photostats for 24 hours and both Tom[150] and I will work on the report tomorrow. J.R.[160]

(160 words)

Typing Drill

(a)	I said I would have it checked.	6
(b)	Some days ago you sent me a long report.	8
(c)	I have asked several of my staff to search for it.	10
(d)	I know it is your custom to photostat your reports.	10

Background Information Exercise — Making erasures

Type one copy of the following, listing the items:

(i) Proof read all work before removing from the typewriter; it is easier to make corrections whilst the work is in the machine. (ii) Do not overtype. (iii) Turn up the platen a few spaces and move the carriage to one side so that rubber dust does not drop into the well of the machine. (iv) Erase carefully so that work is not smudged. (v) Rub gently to avoid damaging the paper. (vi) Use a typewriting rubber but, if the ribbon is new and the type is dark, rub lightly with a soft rubber first.

Production — Memorandum

Use A5 paper turned sideways. Type in fully-blocked style.

Units 1-14

Short Form and Phrase Drill

Dear Sirs ...., months ago ...., I bought ...., large ...., in your ....,

for my ...., for many years ...., according to ...., you can ...., I was ....,

to receive ...., should be glad ...., to let me know ...., has been ....,

Accounts Department ...., Yours faithfully ....

High Frequency Words

two .....2....., number ...., been ...., regular ...., customer ....,

usual ...., practice ...., surprised ...., opportunity ....

Theory — 'R' hook to straight strokes

Brock		Brighton		October		Brett	
Brady		Grayson		Court		daughters	
extremely		records		Grace		Trueman	

Reading — Letter

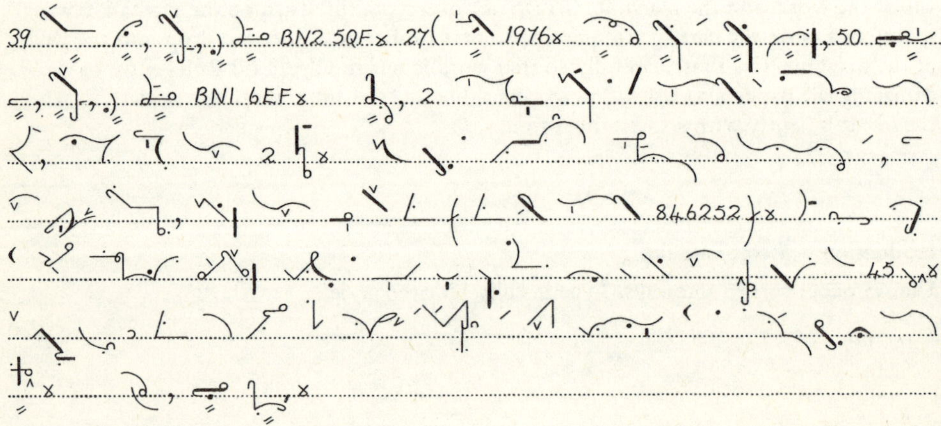

Dictation

39 Brock Lane, Brighton, East Sussex BN2[10] 5QF. 27th October 1976. Messrs.[20] Brett & Brady Limited, 50 Grayson Court, Brighton, East Sussex[30] BN1 6EF. Dear Sirs, Two months[40] ago I bought a large number of garments in your[50] shop, mainly clothing for my two daughters. I have been[60] a regular customer of yours for many years and, according[70] to my usual practice, I paid for my goods by[80] cheque (cheque stub No. 846252).[90] So you can imagine that I was extremely surprised to[100] receive a curt note today asking me to pay my[110] outstanding bill for £45. I should be glad[120] if you would check your records at the earliest opportunity[130] and write to let me know that an error has[140] been made in your Accounts Department. Yours faithfully, Grace Trueman.

(150 words)

Typing Drill

(*a*) Two months ago I bought a large number of garments.   10

(*b*) According to my usual practice, I paid for my goods by cheque.   12

(*c*) I should be glad if you would check your records at the earliest opportunity.   15

Background Information Exercise — Using words accurately

Can you always distinguish between *practice* and *practise*? Type the following sentences and insert the correct word where the dots occur:

(i)   The dentist had such a large practi . . that he engaged another assistant.
(ii)   If you wish to write shorthand at speed you must practi . . daily.
(iii) Do you attend the classes in Office Practi . . ?
(iv)   This has always been my practi . . .
(v)   Practi . . what you preach!

Production — Letter

Use A5 paper. Put Mrs Trueman's address at the top left-hand corner and type the letter in fully-blocked style with open punctuation.

Units 1-14

Short Form and Phrase Drill

in New York ...., in many ...., of our ...., I find ...., that it is ....,

just now ...., of some ...., which are ...., just as ...., and I am ....,

if you will ...., for this ...., to you ...., to be ...., year ...., already ....,

who ...., have you ...., on Monday ...., we can ....

High Frequency Words

November ...., impossible ...., because ...., important ....,

familiar ...., prospect ...., individual ...., members .... ,

February ...., represent ...., come ....

Theory — Intersections

To intersect a single stroke (and circle 's' if appropriate) through another stroke to
represent a complete word is time-saving:

.... for 'business'   our business ....   of our business ....

.... for 'charge'   take charge ....

.... for 'arrangements'   main arrangements ....

.... for 'department'   Sales Department ....   Finance Department ....

                                  Personnel Department ....

Reading — Memo

Dictation

Memo: John Robson to Andrew Bailey. Date it 4th November.[10] Our business in New York, and indeed in many parts[20] of the States, is expanding so rapidly that I am[30] making arrangements for an extensive tour of our American offices.[40] I find that it is impossible for me to leave[50] Head Office just now because of some highly important projects[60] which are pending. You are just as familiar as I[70] am with all aspects of our business and I am[80] asking you if you will take charge of the plans[90] for this visit. Does the prospect of this appeal to[100] you? I intend to invite individual members of each Department[110] to take part and the tour is to be in[120] February next year. I have already decided who should represent[130] the Sales Department and the Finance Department but I am[140] still undecided about the Personnel Department. Have you any suggestions?[150] Can you come to see me early on Monday? We[160] can then discuss some of the main arrangements. J.R.[170]

(170 words)

Typing Drill

(a) Can you come to see me early on Monday?   8

(b) Does the prospect of this appeal to you?   8

(c) I find that it is impossible for me to leave.   9

(d) I am making arrangements for an extensive tour of our American offices.   14

Background Information Exercise — Antonyms

By adding a prefix to some words you can form words of opposite meaning. These are known as *antonyms*. Type the following words in one list and alongside each word type the antonym:

possible, familiar, responsible, valid, modest, agreement, reputable, ethical.

Production — Memorandum

Use A5 paper turned sideways. Put a subject heading 'Tour of American Offices', and type the memorandum in blocked form.

Units 1-14

Short Form and Phrase Drill

subject ...., in the course of the ...., few days ...., and I am pleased ....,

I was ...., particularly ...., I cannot ...., to our ....,

please let me know ...., of this ...., immediately ...., also ....

High Frequency Words

number ...., latest ...., reviews ...., remarks ...., reference ....,

work ....

Theory — Third-place vowels

'ĭ':

Mooney	February	Bill	majority	
extremely	happy	Geography	written	
Minnie	Smith	reprint	History	
recently	published	Economics	Bridges	
if	copy	series	English	

'ŏŏ':

Rook	textbook	books	good	
Booker				

'ēē':

Neil	see	extremely	Sweden	
Vera	reprint	Eileen	recently	
Economics	series			

'ōō':

school	Andrew	Lucas	Ruth	

Reading – Memo

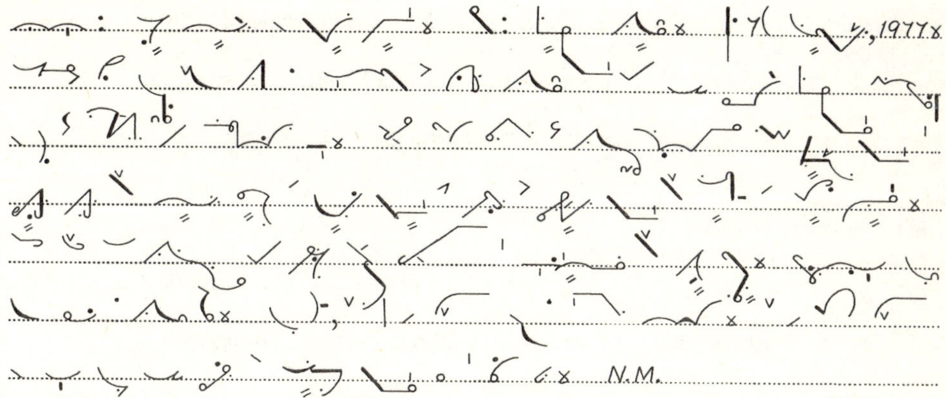

Dictation

Memo: Neil Mooney to Bill Rook. Subject: Textbook Reviews. Date[10] 7th February 1977. In the course of the[20] last few days I have read a number of the[30] latest reviews of our new school textbooks and I am[40] pleased to see that the majority are extremely good. I[50] was particularly happy with the reviewers' remarks about the Geography[60] book on Sweden written by Minnie Smith and Vera Booker[70] and the reprint of the History book by Andrew and[80] Eileen Lucas. I cannot find any reference to our recently[90] published work on Economics by Ruth Bridges. Please let me[100] know if you have seen a review of this. If[110] so, I should like to have a copy immediately. I[120] should also like to know if the new series of[130] English books is on sale yet. N.M.

(138 words)

Typing Drill

(*a*)   I should like to have a copy immediately.   8

(*b*)   I have read a number of the latest reviews of our new school textbooks.   14

Background Information Exercise – Spelling

Words of two syllables ending in 'r' double this 'r' in the present participle and the past tense if the stress is on the second syllable. Type a copy of the following:

| refer | referring | referred | defer | deferring | deferred |
| infer | inferring | inferred | transfer | transferring | transferred |

Production – Memorandum

Use A5 paper turned sideways. Type in blocked form.

Units 1-14

Short Form and Phrase Drill

of years ago .... , to spend .... , with them .... , they arranged .... ,

too much .... , I was .... , particularly .... , thank you .... , with you .... ,

I get .... , I shall be pleased .... , to make arrangements ....

High Frequency Words

June .... , remember .... , near .... , perfect .... , gentle .... ,

walks .... , southern .... , north .... , telegram .... , youngest .... ,

home ....

Theory — Stroke 'z'

Stroke 'z' is used when 'z' is the first or only consonant in a word:

Isaacson ....   Isobel ....   Zurich ....   Zena ....

Stroke 'z' is used when a vowel sound follows 'z' at the end of a word:

Teresa ....   Daisy ....   Pudsey ....   Eliza ....

Circle 's' is written in the middle of an outline for the sound of 'z':

Lausanne ....   Switzerland ....

Reading — Personal letter

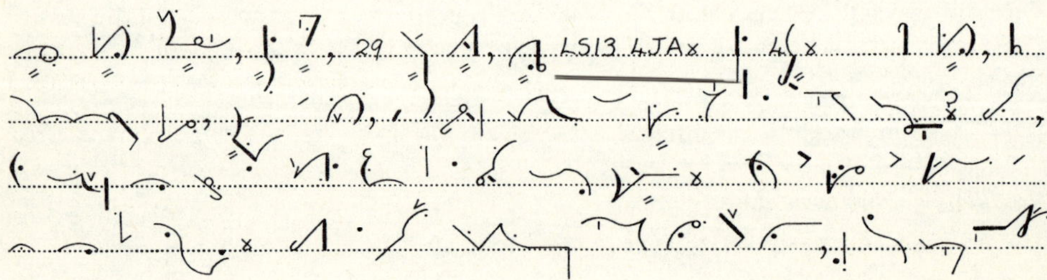

40

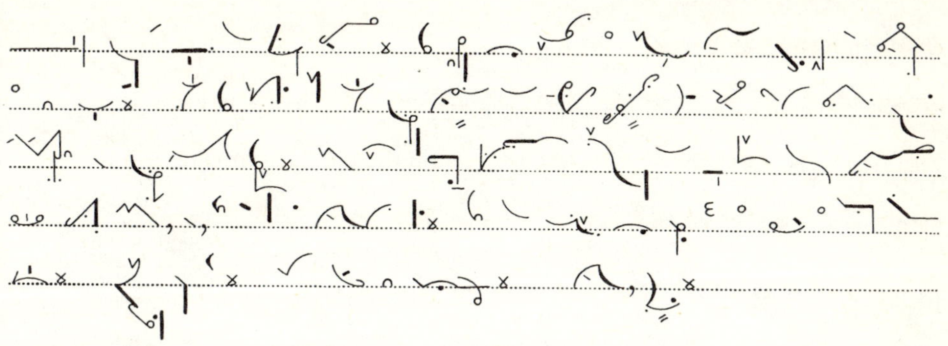

Dictation

Mrs Teresa Isaacson, Daisy Cottage, 29 Pudsey Road, Leeds[10] LS13 4JA. Dated 4th June.[20] Dear Teresa, Do you remember the twins, Isobel and Eliza,[30] who used to live in Italy until a couple of[40] years ago? Well, they invited me to spend a holiday[50] with them at a hotel near Zurich. They arranged all[60] the details of the journey and met me at the[70] airfield. We had a really perfect month lazing by the[80] lake, eating far too much gorgeously cooked food and going[90] for gentle walks. This suited me nicely as I have[100] not long been out of hospital as you know. Until[110] this holiday I had only visited Lausanne in southern Switzerland[120] so I was particularly happy to have an opportunity to[130] visit the north this time. I hope my greetings telegram[140] arrived in good time for your youngest son's wedding and[150] I hope, too, that you all had a lovely day.[160] Thank you for inviting me to stay with you as[170] soon as I get back home. I shall be pleased[180] to do that. I will 'phone you to make arrangements.[190] Love, Zena.

(192 words)

Typing Drill

(*a*) They invited me to spend a holiday with them. 9

(*b*) They arranged all the details of the journey. 9

(*c*) I hope my greetings telegram arrived in good time. 10

Background Information Exercise — Telegrams

Detailed information regarding the sending of telegrams can be found in the *Post Office Guide* which is issued annually by the Post Office. Can you name ten different types of telegram? If not, look in the *Post Office Guide* and make a list.

Production — Personal letter

Use A5 paper and type in indented form. Make five paragraphs.

Units 1-14

Short Form and Phrase Drill

has been .... , to be .... , she will be able to .... , which .... , to make use .... ,

who can .... , always be .... , although .... , but cannot .... , would .... ,

for me .... , first-class .... , in her .... , will be .... , in any office ....

High Frequency Words

short .... , work .... , tried .... , opinion .... , interest .... , during ....

Theory — Diphones (double-vowel signs)

When two vowel sounds follow each other they are shown by the sign ⌐ written in the position of the first vowel sound in the diphone:

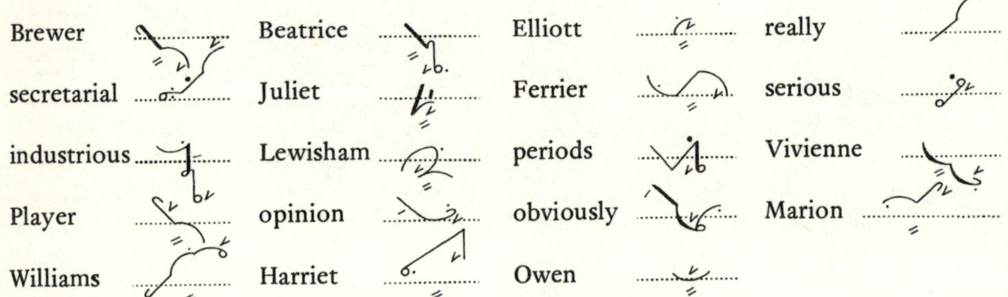

Brewer	Beatrice	Elliott	really
secretarial	Juliet	Ferrier	serious
industrious	Lewisham	periods	Vivienne
Player	opinion	obviously	Marion
Williams	Harriet	Owen	

Reading — Report

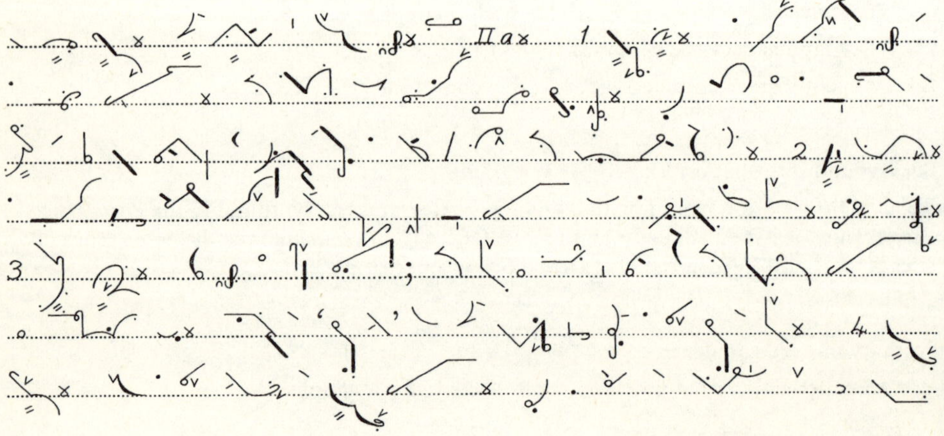

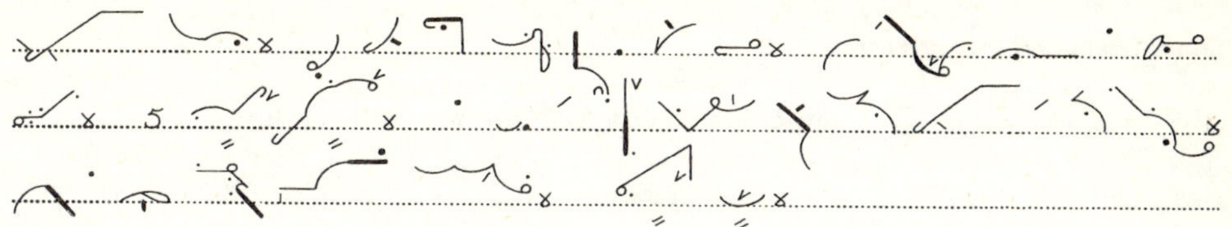

Dictation

To Miss Brewer. Short Report on five students. Class II[10]a. 1 Beatrice Elliott. A really reliable student and an[20] excellent worker. Her ability in the secretarial skills has been[30] outstanding. She also has a good grasp of Spanish and[40] it is to be hoped that she will be able[50] to obtain a post which allows her to make use[60] of this asset. 2 Juliet Ferrier. A girl who can[70] always be relied upon to turn out good work in[80] a reasonably fast time. Serious and industrious. 3 Patricia Lewisham.[90] This student has tried hard; her typing is accurate but[100] slow although her tabular work is extremely neat. Capable of[110] 'speeding up' for short periods but cannot sustain a high[120] speed of typing. 4 Vivienne Player. I have a high[130] opinion of Vivienne's work. She is the sort of person[140] I would pick to work for me. She has shown[150] great interest during the whole course. Will obviously make a[160] first-class secretary. 5 Marion Williams. A neat and tidy[170] person both in her work and her appearance. Will be[180] a most acceptable colleague in any office. Harriet Owen.

(189 words)

Typing Drill

(a)	I have a high opinion of Vivienne's work.	9
(b)	A really reliable student and an excellent worker.	10
(c)	Her ability in the secretarial skills has been outstanding.	12

Background Information Exercise — Diphthongs, triphones and diphones

Type one copy of the following:

DIPHTHONG: A diphthong is two vowel sounds pronounced as one.
TRIPHONE: A triphone is a diphthong plus another following sounded vowel.
DIPHONE: A diphone is two consecutive vowels pronounced in two separate syllables.

Production — Report

Use A4 paper and take a carbon copy. To be sent to Miss Brewer and headed 'Short Report on five students, Class IIa'. Type the students' names in capital letters and block the information under each name. Type Harriet Owen's name at the bottom right-hand corner and put today's date at the left-hand side.

Units 1-14

Short Form and Phrase Drill

dear ......, yesterday ......, Business News ......, at some ......, owe ......,

at the end ......, will you ......, and we hope that ......, for us ......, see you ......,

we were ......, would be ......, how ......, would you ......, with us ......

High Frequency Words

chair ......, important ......, given ......, sufficient ......, coming ......,

great ......, can ......, wishes ......

Theory – Diphthongs 'OW' and 'U'
Diphthong 'OW':

Plough .... Rowntree .... Browning .... Cowley ....

House .... town .... about .... down ....

south .... Fowlers .... Crouch ....

Diphthong 'U':

Kew .... Hugh .... View .... Newby ....

newspaper .... Tuesday .... Dewberry .... Newman ....

news .... Muriel ....

Reading – Personal letter

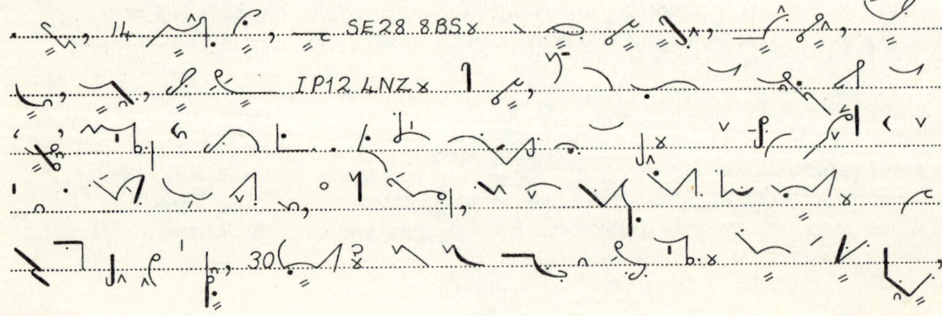

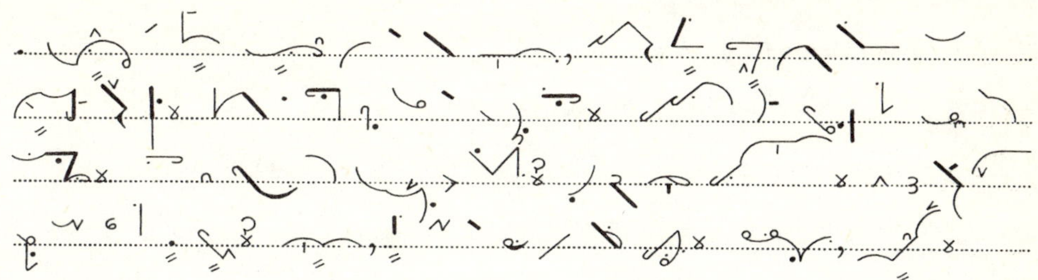

Dictation

The Plough, 14 Rowntree Lane, Kew SE28[10] 8BS. To Mr. Hugh Browning, Cowley House, Forest[20] View, Newby, West Suffolk IP12 4N[30]Z. Dear Hugh, I saw your name in the newspaper[40] yesterday in the 'Business News' and I noticed that you[50] were taking the chair at some important meeting in town.[60] I suddenly realized that I owe you an apology for[70] not writing to you, as I had promised, about my[80] birthday party at the end of March. Will you be[90] able to get down south on Tuesday, 30th March? I[100] hope I have given you sufficient notice. Pam and Gerry[110] Dewberry, the Fowlers and Tom Newman will all be coming,[120] and we hope that Jack Crouch will be back in[130] London by that date. It will be a great treat[140] for us all to see you again. We were so[150] pleased at the news of your engagement. Can you bring[160] your fiancée to the party? She would be most welcome.[170] How would you both like to stay the night with[180] us at The Plough? Mum, Dad and I all send[190] our best wishes. Sincerely, Muriel.

(195 words)

Typing Drill

(*a*) We were so pleased at the news of your engagement.   10

(*b*) It will be a great pleasure for us all to see you again.   11

(*c*) You were taking the chair at some important meeting in town.   12

Background Information Exercise — Accents and 'dead keys'

Type one copy of the following:

The acute accent must be inserted in the word 'fiancée'. Some typewriters have fitted keys for the four French accents — acute (´), grave (`), cedilla (¸), and circumflex (^). These are known as 'dead keys' because the carriage does not move along one space when the accents are typed. The accent is typed first and the letter afterwards. If the typewriter does not have any accent keys, the accents must be inserted on the work in ink.

Production — Personal letter

Use A5 paper and insert a suitable date. Block the addresses but use indented form for the letter. Remember to put the acute accent (´) on the first 'e' of 'fiancée'.

Units 1-14

Short Form and Phrase Drill

10th June ......, I have no doubt ......, that you will ......, have made ......,

full arrangements ......, produce the ......, price list ......, all our ......,

which is ......, weeks' time ......, should be glad ......, with the ......, I am ......,

that this ......, at the same time ......, your Department ......, has been ......,

if this is ......, I will ......, if he can ......, please do not ......,

to let me know ......

High Frequency Words

dated ......, principal ......, products ......, certain ......, told ......, behind ......,

schedule ......, urgent ......, regard ......, despatch ......, middle ......

Theory — First- and third-place diphthongs

First-place 'I' and 'OI':

Ivor	......	Bright	......	Caroline	......	Simons	......
litho	......	trying	......	Roy	......	my	......
right	......	July	......				

Third-place 'OW' and 'U':

new	......	due	......	about	......	out	......
issue	......	down	......				

Note: Where a final diphthong is joined to a single stroke, the stroke may be halved to indicate a final 't' or 'd'.

Reading — Memo

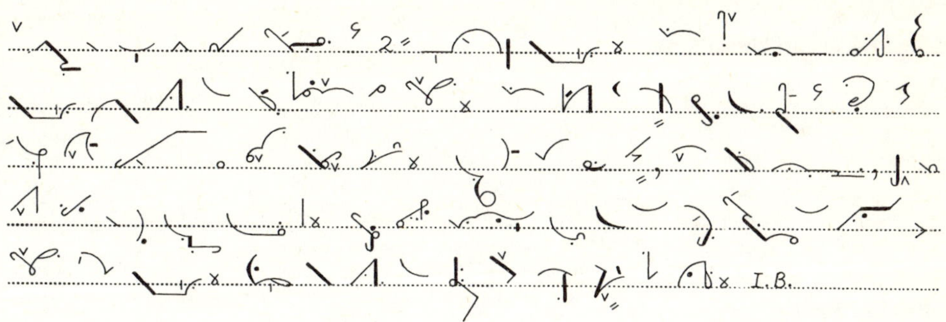

Dictation

Memo: Ivor Bright to Caroline Simons. Dated 10th June. I[10] have no doubt that you will have made full arrangements[20] to produce the off-set litho copies of the new[30] price list for all our principal products which is due[40] to be issued in about four weeks' time but I[50] should be glad to know how you are progressing with[60] the two-coloured booklet. I am trying to make certain[70] that this booklet will be ready for posting at the[80] same time as the price list. I am told that[90] your Department has been having trouble with the machines and[100] that the off-set litho work is slightly behind schedule.[110] If this is so I will send Roy, my best[120] mechanic, down to you right away to see if he[130] can fix it. Please do not hesitate to let me[140] know if you have any urgent problems in regard to[150] the price list or the booklet. They must be ready[160] for despatch by the middle of July at the latest.[170] I.B.

(172 words)

Typing Drill

(*a*) I should be glad to know how you are progressing. 10

(*b*) The off-set litho work is slightly behind schedule. 10

(*c*) Please do not hesitate to let me know if you have any urgent problems. 14

Background Information Exercise — Using words accurately

Can you always distinguish between *principal* and *principle*? Type the following sentences and insert the correct word where the dots occur:

(i)   The Princip . . of the College called an urgent meeting.
(ii) This was the princip . . cause of the trouble.
(iii) I abstained from voting on princip . . .
(iv) The President of the Association was the princip . . speaker.

Production — Memorandum

Use A5 paper turned sideways. Insert a suitable subject heading and type in blocked style.

Units 1-14

Short Form and Phrase Drill

have just ...., towards the ...., of last ...., particularly ...., if you will be
able to ...., with us ...., of course ...., but we ...., don't be ....,
I am not ...., ask you ...., things ...., eye ...., to tell ...., I can ....

High Frequency Words

Miss ...., most ...., southern ...., hard ...., help ...., house ....,
whole ...., colours ...., phone ....

Theory — Triphones

Diana ...., Howard ...., Royal ...., Brierley ....

Brian ...., enjoyable ...., voyage ...., via ....

genuine ...., valuable ...., variety ...., Samuel ....

Reading — Personal letter

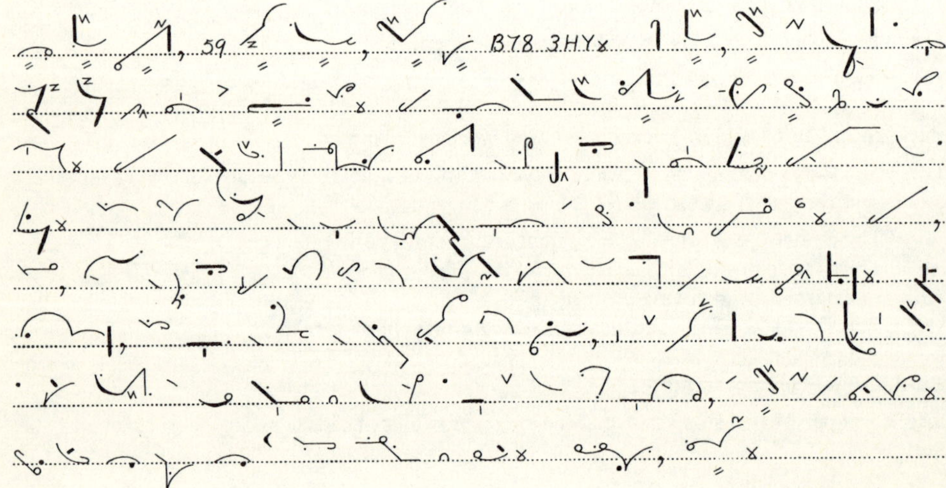

Dictation

Miss Diana Howard, 59 Royal Avenue, Brierley Hill B[10]78 3HY. Dear Diana, Brian and I[20] have just had a most enjoyable voyage round some of[30] the Greek islands. We came back via Sardinia and southern[40] Spain towards the end of last month. We are both[50] finding it extremely hard to settle down again to do[60] some genuine work for a change. I am particularly anxious[70] to know if you will be able to come and[80] spend a few weeks with us. We are, of course,[90] longing to see you again but we also want your[100] valuable help in getting our new house decorated. Don't be[110] alarmed, I am not going to ask you to paper[120] the walls or ceiling, but I really do need your[130] advice on buying a whole variety of things because you[140] have such a good eye for matching colours, and Brian[150] and I are hopeless. Please phone me to tell me[160] that I can expect you soon. Sincerely, Samuel.

(168 words)

Typing Drill

(*a*) We came back via Sardinia and southern Spain.   10

(*b*) Please phone me to tell me that I can expect you soon.   11

(*c*) We are both finding it extremely hard to settle down again.   12

Background Information Exercise — Spelling

The following words all end in 'ible' or 'able'. Type them in a single list, in alphabetical order:

enjoy . . . .   cred . . . .   leg . . . .   credit . . . .   desir . . . .   poss . . . .

neglig . . . .   indel . . . .   indispens . . . .   infall . . . .   laugh . . . .

destruct . . . .

Production

Type the letter on A5 paper and put a date some time in June. Type in indented style and put the address at the bottom of the letter.

Units 1-14

Short Form and Phrase Drill

all ...., particularly ...., to get the ...., would you ...., at once ....,

entry forms ...., that they ...., to receive the ...., some time ....,

this is the ....

High Frequency Words

people ...., beginning ...., numbers .... them ...., tell ...., can ....,

expect ...., next ...., cheques ....

Theory — Upward 'h'
The sound of 'h' is represented by .... written upwards .... :

Hooper	Hardy	happy	Hunt ....
Highway	Hastings	Henry	Hutton ....
Hythe	Hayes	Harriet	Hancock ....
Hoxton	Havant	Hicks	Hobbs ....
Hinton	Hester	Hodge	Heydon ....

Reading — Memo

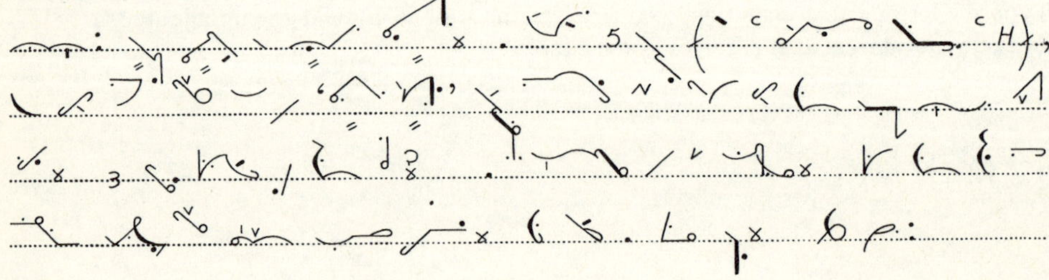

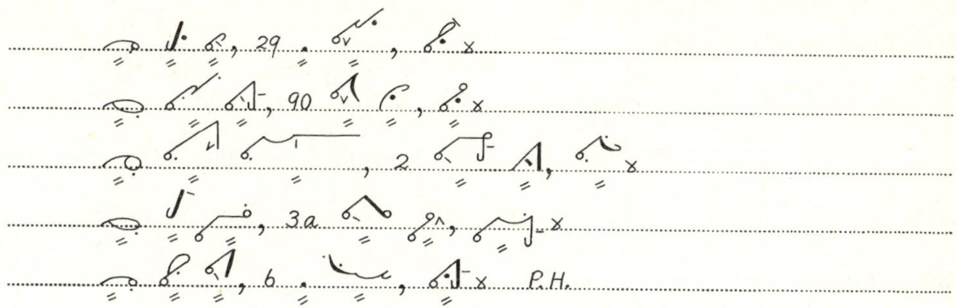

Dictation

Memo: Peter Hooper to Mary Hardy. The following 5 people[10] (all with surnames beginning with H), have won cash prizes[20] in our 'Happy Holiday' publicity campaign and I particularly want[30] them to get the money right away. Would you please[40] telephone each of them at once? The numbers are on[50] the entry forms. Tell them that they can expect to[60] receive the prize some time next week. Then post the[70] cheques today. This is the list: Miss Jane Hunt, 29[80] The Highway, Hastings. Mr Henry Hutton, 90 Hythe Lane,[90] Hayes. Mrs Harriet Hancock, 2 Hoxton Road, Havant. Mr John[100] Hicks, 3a Hobbs House, Hinton. Miss Hester Hodge, 6[110] The Avenue, Heydon. P.H.

(115 words)

Typing Drill

(*a*) The numbers are on the entry forms.   7

(*b*) Would you please telephone them at once?   8

(*c*) The following 5 people have won cash prizes.   9

Background Information Exercise — Addressing envelopes

Using open punctuation, type each of the addresses from the Dictation passage as they would appear on an envelope. The Counties are, in order: East Sussex TN35 4HR, Kent TN12 0EB, Hampshire PO9 2LH, South Herefordshire HR2 8JQ and Norfolk NR11 6RB.

Production — Memorandum

Use A5 paper turned sideways and insert today's date. Type in fully-blocked style and put a suitable subject heading.

Units 1-14

Short Form and Phrase Drill

Dear Madam .... , thank you .... , as we are having .... , this will .... , in the meantime .... , which will .... , with us .... , large .... , of these .... , can be .... , in fact .... , several .... , we shall be .... , hours .... , Yours faithfully ....

High Frequency Words

telephone .... , call .... , perhaps .... , care .... , inspect ....

Theory — Tick 'h'

The sound of 'h' occurring before 'm', upward 'l', and downward 'r' at the beginning of a word is represented by a light tick written downwards from right to left:

Before 'm':

Ham .... Homes ....

Before upward 'l':

Helen .... Hill .... Holiday .... help ....

Hilton ....

Before downward 'r':

Hurst .... hire .... here ....

Reading — Letter

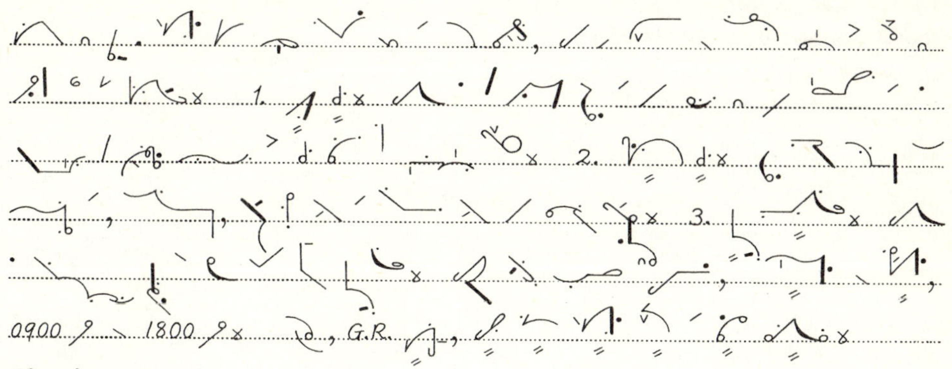

Dictation

Mrs Helen Harvey, 90 Hurst Crescent, Forest Hill, London S[10]E25 6XW. Dear Madam, Thank you[20] for your telephone call about our full hire service for[30] tents, trailer tents and touring caravans. Perhaps you would care[40] to visit us here at West Ham one day next[50] week and inspect our goods as we are having a[60] 'Holiday Homes Week' with all our models on display. This[70] will show you the range and scope of our goods.[80] In the meantime, to help you choose the holiday which[90] will most appeal to you and your husband, we should[100] like to answer some of the points you raised with[110] us on the telephone. 1. Ridge Tents. We have a[120] large range of these and are sending you our stocklist[130] and a booklet which illustrates many of the tents selling[140] at economy prices. 2. Trailer Tents. These can be erected[150] in minutes and, in fact, both setting up and packing[160] up are simple procedures. 3. Touring Caravans. We have a[170] permanent display of several of our top touring vans. We[180] shall be open next week, Monday to Saturday, 0900[190] hours to 1800 hours. Yours faithfully, G. R. Hilton,[200] West Ham Holiday Hire and Sales Service.

(207 words)

Typing Drill

(*a*) Thank you for your telephone call.   7

(*b*) Perhaps you would care to visit us here at West Ham one day next week.   14

Background Information Exercise — Pairs of words

Type sentences to show the correct use of the following pairs of words:

illustrated,	illuminated	superb,	supreme
reproduction,	repetition	retire,	retreat

Production — Letter

Use A4 paper and take a carbon copy. Date the letter 27th February. Type in blocked style and itemise the three points mentioned. Leave sufficient space for a signature.

Units 1-14

Theory — Upward and Downward 'l'

Stroke 'l' is usually written upward:

long		elephant		bill		lion	
Elizabeth		Leicester		village		Solomon's	
loved		gaslight		small		pavilions	

but 'l' is written downward:

after 'n':	only		O'Neill		Nelson
after 'n' halved:	until		recently		
after 'ng':	Kingley				

Reading — Book list

1		9	
2		10	
3		11	
4		12	
5		13	
6		14	
7		15	
8		16	

54

Dictation

1. The Long Memory
2. Elephant Bill
3. The Year of the Lion
4. Elizabeth and Leicester
5. Only Two Can Play
6. Village Diary
7. King Solomon's Ring
8. The Kingley Papers
9. The Loved and Envied
10. Fanny by Gaslight
11. Until I Came
12. Recently in Rome
13. Major O'Neill
14. The Small Back Room
15. Nelson
16. The Bright Pavilions

Typing Drill

(*a*) KING SOLOMON'S RING   4

(*b*) THE LOVED AND ENVIED   4

(*c*) E L E P H A N T   B I L L   5

(*d*) T H E   Y E A R   O F   T H E   L I O N   8

Background Information Exercise — Book titles

Type a copy of the following:

Titles of books appearing in a manuscript may be:

(i)   enclosed in quotation marks — 'The Small Back Room'; or

(ii) typed in lower case without quotation marks and underscored — <u>The Small Back Room</u>; or

(iii) typed in upper-case characters — THE SMALL BACK ROOM.

Production — Book list

Type on A5 paper. Using double spacing, type the book list in alphabetical order. (The order of words in each title is to be exactly preserved.)

Units 1-14

Short Form and Phrase Drill

I am certain ...., that this is the ...., Export Department ...., to take ....,

if we can ...., it is certain ...., that you will be able to ....,

three weeks ...., should be glad ...., to discuss the ...., of your

Department ...., let me have ....

High Frequency Words

during ...., spirit ...., opportunity ...., most ...., hard ....,

important ....

Theory — 'N' hook
An 'n' hook is written:
inside curves:

Len .... fine .... within ....

clockwise to straight strokes:

Batten .... John .... Hutton .... Eastern ....

Western .... gone .... maintain .... European ....

burden .... town .... return .... down ....

in the middle of a word:
memorandum .... unfortunately ....

Reading — Memo

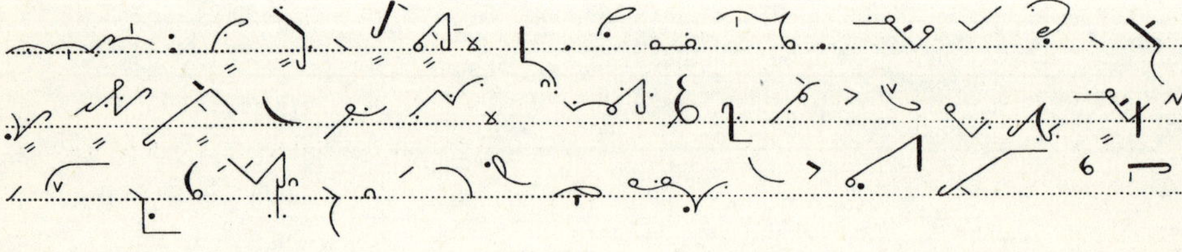

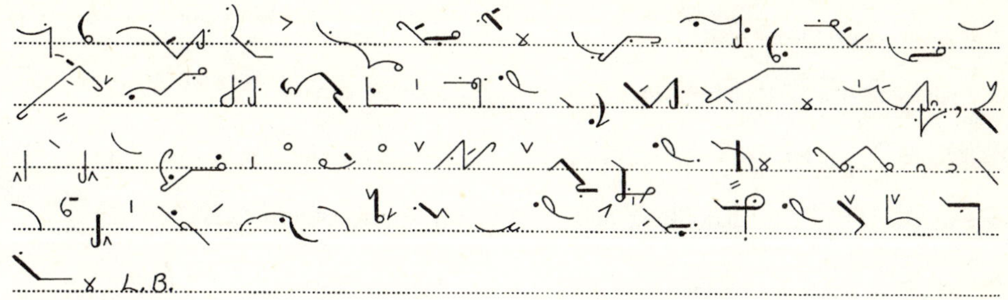

Dictation

Memorandum: Len Batten to John Hutton. During the last six[10] months the exports of our machines to both Eastern and[20] Western Europe have risen rapidly. I am certain that this[30] is the direct result of the fine spirit within the[40] Export Department and I should like to take this opportunity[50] to thank you and your staff most sincerely for all[60] the hard work that has gone into this important aspect[70] of the firm's progress abroad. If we can maintain these[80] export figures in European markets it is certain that you[90] will be able to take on extra staff to ease[100] the burden of work. Unfortunately, I shall be out of[110] town for three weeks but as soon as I return[120] I should be glad to discuss the staffing of your[130] Department. Perhaps you would put your thoughts down on paper[140] and let me have your ideas about new staff and[150] the upgrading of existing staff by the time I get[160] back. L.B.

(163 words)

Typing Drill

(a) Unfortunately, I shall be out of town for three weeks. 10

(b) I should be glad to discuss the staffing of your Department. 12

(c) Exports of our machines to both Eastern and Western Europe have risen rapidly. 16

Background Information Exercise — Antonyms

By adding a prefix to some words you can form words of opposite meaning. These are known as *antonyms*. Type the following words in one list and alongside each word type the antonym:

> sincere, important, fortunate, order, perfect, dependence, charitable, discretion.

Production — Memorandum

Use A5 paper turned sideways and take a carbon copy. Put today's date and use blocked style.

Units 1-14

Short Form and Phrase Drill

and we think it is ...., for which you are ...., we are sorry ....,

so long ...., it has not been ...., years ...., can be seen ...., anytime ....,

and we suggest ...., that you should ...., early arrangements ....,

for we feel ...., that it will not be ...., Yours sincerely ....

High Frequency Words

Mr ...., Messrs ...., property ...., modern ...., garden ...., market ....

Theory — Circles and loops to 'n' hook

Clarence	Jones	Spence	Gibbons ....
Barons	Dunster	Robins	Burns ....
Chance	Agents		

Reading — Letter

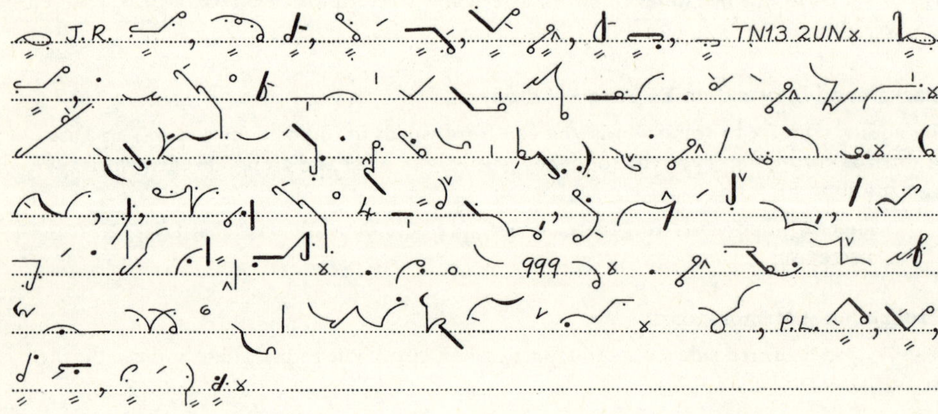

Dictation

Mr J. R. Clarence, Messrs Jones, Spence & Gibbons, Barons[10] House, Dunster Green, Kent TN13 2U[20]N. Dear Mr Clarence, A new property has just come[30] on to our books and we think it is exactly[40] the sort of house for which you are looking. We[50] are sorry to have been so long in obtaining a[60] suitable place for you but it has not been easy[70] to find a house which fits all your needs. This[80] lovely, detached, centrally heated property has four good-size bedrooms,[90] spacious lounge and dining room, large modern kitchen and a[100] well laid-out garden. The lease is for 999[110] years. The house can be seen anytime and we[120] suggest that you should make early arrangements with us to[130] view it for we feel that it will not be[140] long on the market. Yours sincerely, P. L. Robins, Burns,[150] Chance & Grey, Land and Estate Agents.

(157 words)

Typing Drill

(a)	The house can be seen anytime.	6
(b)	A new property has just come on to our books.	9
(c)	For we feel that it will not be long on the market.	10

Background Information Exercise — Using the ampersand

The abbreviated form of 'and' — the ampersand '&' — may be used in a firm's title, e.g.

Jones, Spence & Gibbons
Burns, Chance & Grey

but this abbreviated form is never typed in the body of a letter. It may sometimes be used, however, when typing in a very restricted space, e.g. a heading on a small filing card or index card. Make up and TYPE some names of firms, using the ampersand.

Production — Letter

Use A5 paper and date the letter today. Type in fully-blocked style and take a carbon copy.

Units 1-14

Short Form and Phrase Drill

subject ...., several ...., to this Company ...., particularly ...., last few ....,

also been ...., I think we may ...., think that the ...., necessary arrange-

ments ...., accordingly ...., he has arranged ...., and I hope you will ....,

if you will not be ...., Personnel Department ...., Accounts Department ....,

Export Department ...., Sales Department ....

High Frequency Words

March ...., regard ...., during ...., been ...., neglecting ....,

Board ....

Theory — Suffixes 'ment' and 'ly'

The suffix 'ment' is sometimes written ....,
    joined to the preceding stroke: recruitment ....

To make an easier joining, the suffix
    'ment' is sometimes written ....:   Department ....   appointments ....

The suffix 'ly' is sometimes joined to the
    preceding stroke: Manley ....   lately ....

A disjoined upward 'l' is sometimes used
    for the suffix 'ly':   urgently ....   certainly ....

Reading — Memo

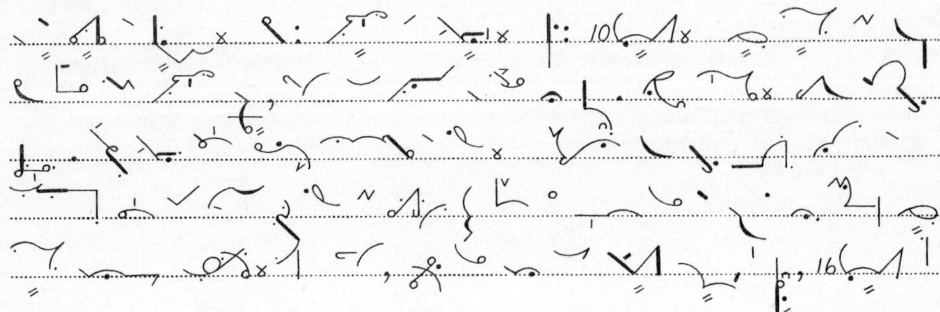

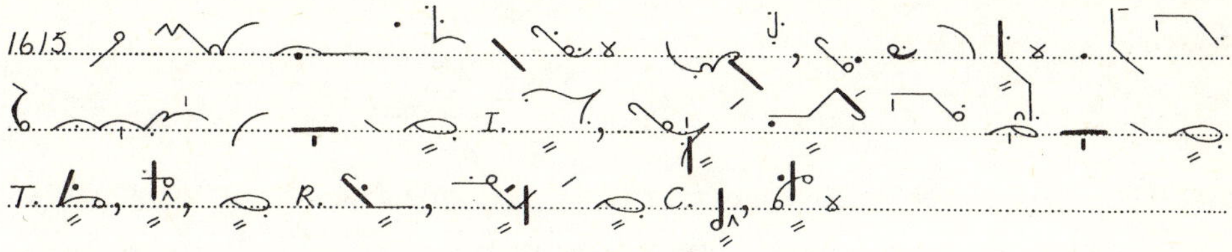

Dictation

To All Heads of Department. Subject: Recruitment and Upgradings. Date:[10] 10th March. Mr Manley and I have had several talks[20] about recruitment to this Company, particularly in regard to appointments[30] made during the last few months. We have also been[40] discussing the possible upgrading of some senior members of staff.[50] I think we may have been guilty lately of neglecting[60] some of our long established staff and I certainly think[70] that the time has come for us all to have[80] a meeting and I asked Mr Manley to make the[90] necessary arrangements. Accordingly, he has arranged for us to meet[100] in the Board Room on Tuesday, 16th March at 1615[110] hours and I hope you will make an attempt[120] to be present. If you will not be attending, please[130] send your Deputy. The top copy of this memorandum will[140] go to Mr I. Manley, Personnel Department and carbon copies[150] must go to Mr T. James, Accounts Department, Mr R.[160] Blake, Export Department and Mr C. Downs, Sales Department.

(169 words)

Typing Drill

(*a*) Mr Ian Manley and I have had several talks about recruitment.   13

(*b*) I certainly think that the time has come for us all to have a meeting.   14

Background Information Exercise — Multiple carbons

Type a copy of the following. When a memorandum is being sent to more than one person the names of the recipients may be typed in the heading:

To: Mr I Manley
Mr T James
Mr R Blake
Mr C Downs

and the person for whom each carbon is intended will have his name ticked or underlined. Alternatively, the distribution list may be given at the base of the memorandum or even on a separate sheet if there are many names.

Production — Memorandum

Use A5 paper turned sideways. Type in blocked style and take four carbon copies (one for the file copy). Put the distribution list at the base of the memo.

Units 1-17

Short Form and Phrase Drill

Dear Mr ...., we very much ...., from your ...., yesterday ...., that the
goods ...., we sent ...., have not yet ...., you should ...., it is possible ....,
I can ...., that these goods ...., have been ...., if you have ...., or so ....,
and we will ...., of course ...., to send you ...., without delay ....,
Yours sincerely ...., Sales Manager ....

High Frequency Words

certainly ...., everything ...., special ...., however ...., instruct ....

Theory — 'r' hook to curves

A small hook written inside and at the beginning of a curved stroke adds the sound of
'r':

Trevor	....	Freeman	....	Manor	....	Dover	....
Friday	....	through	....	Francis	....	Overton	....
Frank	....	French	....				

Reading — Letter

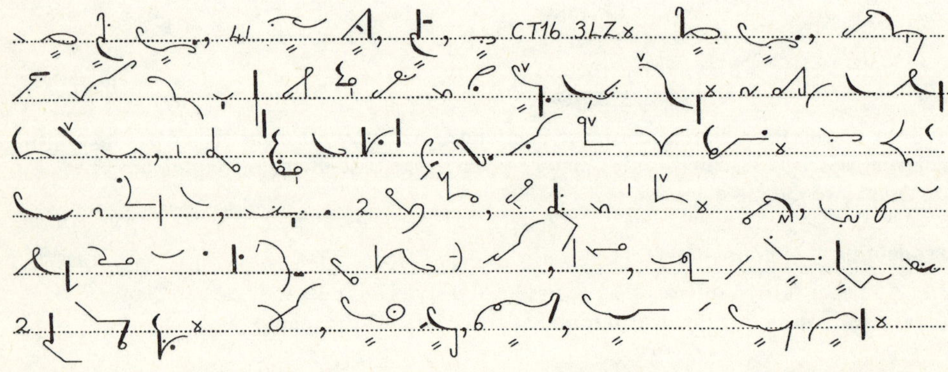

Dictation

To Mr Trevor Freeman, 41 Manor Road, Dover, Kent[10] CT16 3LZ. Dear Mr Freeman,[20] We very much regret to learn from your note dated[30] yesterday that the goods we sent to you last Friday[40] have not yet arrived. You should certainly have received them[50] by now, but it is possible that these goods have[60] been delayed through the brief rail strike early this week.[70] I can assure you that everything you asked for, including[80] the two special items, was despatched to you on time.[90] However, if you have still not received the articles in[100] a day or so please telephone us and we will,[110] of course, instruct our Packing Department to send you two[120] duplicate packages without delay. Yours sincerely, Francis Overton, Sales Manager,[130] Frank and French Limited.

(134 words)

Typing Drill

(*a*) We regret to learn that the goods have not yet arrived.   11

(*b*) I can assure you that everything was despatched to you.   11

(*c*) We will, of course, instruct our Packing Department to send you two duplicate packages.   18

Background Information Exercise — Use of words: 'special' and 'especial'

You need to become familiar with commonly used books of reference. One of these is *Fowler's Modern English Usage.* Borrow this book from your library (or office practice room), turn to the word *especial(ly)* and read the first paragraph which gives an explanation of the distinction between *special* and *especial*.

Production — Letter

Type the letter on A5 paper and put today's date. Type the addressee in blocked form and the text in indented style. Leave sufficient space for a signature and centre '(Francis Overton)' and 'Frank and French Limited' under 'Yours sincerely'.

Units 1-17

Short Form and Phrase Drill

over the ...., before ...., I left ...., putting ...., it will not be ...., anyway ...., and I am ...., there is ...., number of ...., I think ...., more ...., anybody ...., would you ...., for some time ....

High Frequency Words

weekend ...., lovely ...., country ...., suddenly ...., remembered ...., advertisement ...., much ...., appointment ...., next ...., wish ....

Theory — Reverse forms 'fer', 'ver', 'ther', 'THer'

'Fer, 'ver', 'ther' and 'THer' are always reversed after horizontal strokes and upstrokes:

Silverman .... Clover .... Witherley .... Waverley ....

Heather .... Oliver .... Glover .... river ....

Kathryn ....

Reading — Personal letter

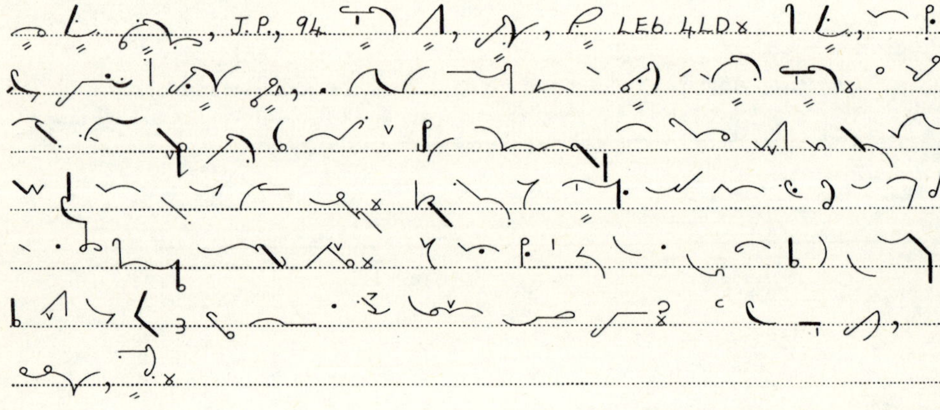

Dictation

Miss Jenny Silverman, J.P., 94 Clover Road, Witherley,[10] Leicester LE6 4LD. Dear Jenny, I[20] am staying over the week-end at Waverley House, the lovely[30] country home of Heather and Oliver Glover. As I was[40] ambling along beside the river this morning I suddenly remembered[50] my promise to write to you before I left about[60] the advertisement I am putting in the local newspaper. It[70] will not be appearing un-til Monday anyway and I am[80] afraid there is not much chance of a tremendous number[90] of replies. I think I may stay on here for[100] a few more days so if anybody does write for[110] the job would you please make an appointment for some[120] time next week? With every good wish, Sincerely, Kathryn.

(129 words)

Typing Drill

(*a*) I am staying over the weekend.	6
(*b*) I was ambling along beside the river this morning.	10
(*c*) There is not much chance of a tremendous number of replies.	12

Background Information Exercise — Abbreviations

Can you give the full-length form for the following abbreviations? Type in one list, in alphabetical order, and add the full form beside each one:

UNESCO   JP   OBE   BBC   COD   WHO   UNO
RSPCC   GC   MS

Production — Personal letter

Type the letter on A5 paper, in fully-blocked style with open punctuation. Date the letter 29 November.

Units 1-17

Short Form and Phrase Drill

so much .... , I am very sorry .... , long time .... , thanking .... , thank

you .... , few days .... , difficulty .... , until the .... , from my .... , I am

certain .... , I hope .... , I shall be able to ....

High Frequency Words

pleasure .... , however .... , expecting .... , insisted ....

Theory — Hooks 'n', 'f' and 'v' in phrasing

Hook 'n':

more than ....   to have ....   better than ....   I had been ....
                        been

earlier than ....

Hook 'f':

number of ....   out of ....   in spite of ....   instead of ....
                                    the

Hook 'v':

who have ....
   been

Reading — Personal letter

Dictation

Greystoke Hospital, Manchester M24 3GP. 29th[10] March. Dear Frances, More than a week has gone[20] by since you sent me those gorgeous flowers which gave[30] me so much pleasure. I am very sorry to have[40] been such a terribly long time in thanking you. However,[50] as I am now much better than I was, I[60] am sitting up in bed typing a number of 'thank[70] you' notes to my friends who have been so kind[80] and showered me with presents. I think I shall be[90] out of hospital in a few days in spite of[100] the difficulty I shall have hopping about until the plaster[110] is removed from my leg. I had been expecting my[120] discharge from hospital earlier than this; instead of which my[130] ankle began to swell up and they insisted that I[140] had an X-ray taken of my foot. I am[150] certain that I shall be back in my flat by[160] the weekend. I hope I shall be able to see[170] you soon. Love, Doris.

(174 words)

Typing Drill

(*a*) I think I shall be out of hospital in a few days. 10

(*b*) More than a week has gone by since you sent me those gorgeous flowers. 14

(*c*) I am very sorry to have been such a terribly long time in thanking you. 14

Background Information Exercise — Pairs of words

Using your dictionary look up the exact meanings of the following pairs of words. When you are sure that you know the difference between the words, type sentences to show their correct use:

insisted	persisted	consigned	assigned
precise	accurate	substitute	deputy

Production — Personal letter

Use A5 paper and type in indented form. Make five paragraphs.

Units 1-17

Short Form and Phrase Drill

subject ...., I have now ...., all our ...., commercial ...., this is ....,

to take place ...., next month ...., will have ...., long way ....,

but those ...., from the ...., to be ...., should be ...., initial arrangements ....,

I hope ...., to be able to ...., many thanks ...., few days ....

High Frequency Words

representatives ...., general ...., northern ...., southern ...., short ....,

organize ...., people ...., give ....

Theory — 'L' hook to curves

A large hook written at the beginning of a curved stroke adds the sound of 'l':

Flagg .... Ethel .... Flaxton .... official ....

approval .... travel .... relatively .... grateful ....

initial ....

Reading — Memo

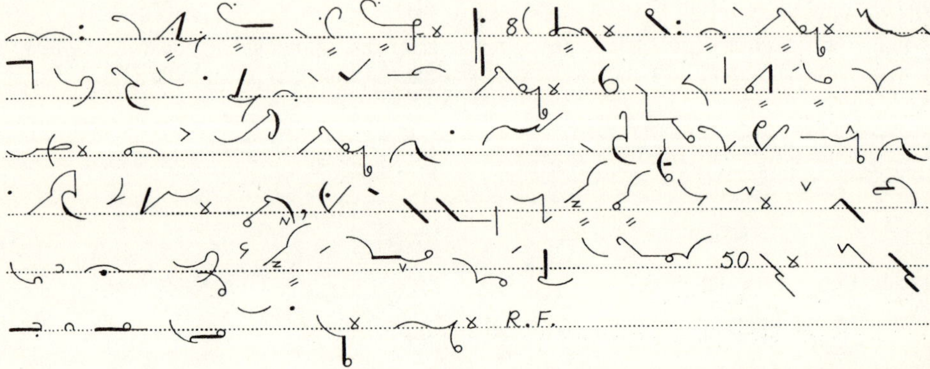

Dictation

Memo: From Reginald Flagg to Ethel Flaxton. Dated 8th December.[10] Subject: Meeting of Representatives. I have now got official approval[20] for a general meeting of all our commercial representatives. This[30] is to take place here at Head Office early next[40] month. Some of the northern representatives will have a long[50] way to travel but those from the southern counties will[60] have a relatively short journey. However, they are all to[70] be booked into the Royal Hotel for the night. I[80] should be grateful if you would make initial arrangements with[90] the Royal and organize rooms and dinner for approximately 50[100] people. I hope to be able to give you exact[110] figures in a few days. Many thanks. R.F.

(119 words)

Typing Drill

(*a*) I have now got official approval for a general meeting. 11

(*b*) This is to take place here at Head Office early next month. 12

(*c*) I should be grateful if you would make initial arrangements. 12

Background Information Exercise — Antonyms

Type the following words in one list and alongside each word type its antonym:

grateful, organize, probable, religious, truth, visible, seemly, consistent, penetrable.

Production — Memorandum

Type the memo on A5 paper, turned sideways. Centre the subject heading and type in indented style.

Units 1-17

Short Form and Phrase Drill

I have had .... , first .... , I was .... , at first .... , well-known .... ,

from .... , I can .... , at last .... , to come .... , on Saturday .... ,

having .... , there will be .... , of us .... , altogether .... , and if we find .... ,

there ....

High Frequency Words

Mr .... , rather .... , because .... , highly .... , respected .... , never .... ,

believed .... , published .... , told .... , call .... , over ....

Theory — Reverse forms of 'fl' and 'vl'

The reverse forms of 'fl' and 'vl' are always used after upstrokes and horizontal strokes:

Lovell .... Yeovil .... marvellous .... novel ....

Revell .... Wavell .... novelist .... Dragonfly ....

Reading — Personal letter

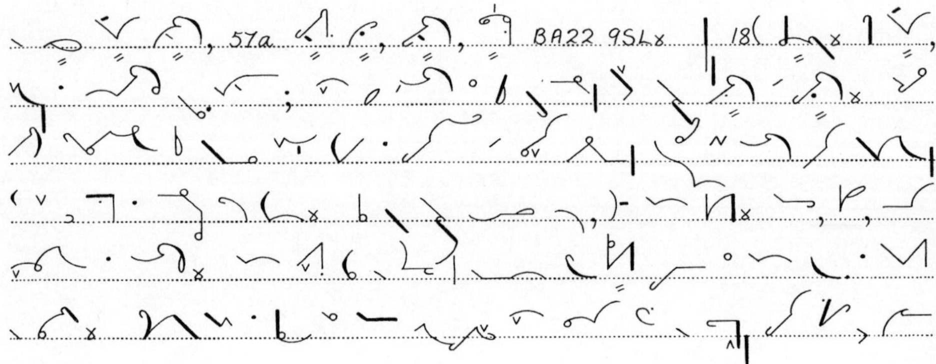

Dictation

To Mr Paul Lovell, 57a Watery Lane, Yeovil,[10] Somerset BA22 9SL. Dated 18th[20] December. Dear Paul, I have had a marvellous piece of[30] luck; my first novel has just been accepted by the[40] publishers Revell & Wavell. I was rather apprehensive at first[50] because I know they are a well-known and highly[60] respected firm and I never really believed that I would[70] get an acceptance from them. It is to be published[80] next year, so I am told. I can, at last,[90] call myself a novelist. I am writing this to ask[100] you to come over on Saturday week as I am[110] having a party to celebrate. There will be about a[120] dozen of us altogether and if we find my small[130] flat too crowded we will adjourn to the local inn,[140] the 'Dragonfly'. So if you arrive to discover that the[150] flat is uninhabited come on down to join us there.[160] See you then. Sincerely, John.

(165 words)

Typing Drill

(*a*)	My first novel has just been accepted.	8
(*b*)	It is to be published next year, so I am told.	9
(*c*)	I know they are a well-known and highly respected firm.	11

Background Information Exercise — Use of words

Type the following phrases and beside each type a single word which has the same meaning.

(i) not lived in (U);
(ii) declining in value (D);
(iii) becoming worse in quality (D);
(iv) never making a mistake (I);
(v) delicately constructed and easily broken (F).

Production — Personal letter

Type the letter on A5 paper. Put your own address at the top right-hand corner. Put the addressee's name and address at the bottom left-hand corner. Type in blocked form.

Units 1-17

Short Form and Phrase Drill

how .... , just now .... , difficulty .... , of last month .... , that .... , I thought .... ,

have no .... , I find .... , very .... , any .... , kind enough .... , or so ....

High Frequency Words

greatest .... , possible .... , reading .... , meeting .... , were .... , sure ....

Theory — Hooks 'f' and 'v'

A small hook written at the end of a straight stroke (on the circle 's' side) adds the sound of 'f' or 'v' in the middle of an outline, or at the end of an outline if there is no following vowel:

In the middle:

David ....   definitely ....   defective ....   Daphne ....

devote ....

At the end:

Cuff ....   Geoff ....   Grove ....   forgive ....

brief ....   rough ....   positive ....   deserve ....

observed ....   effective ....   half ....

Reading — Memo

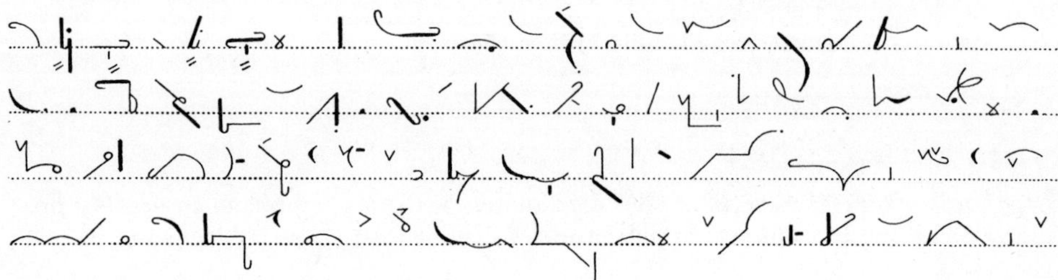

Dictation

From David Cuff to Geoff Grove. Do forgive me for[10] bothering you for I know how busy you are just[20] now but I am having the greatest possible difficulty in[30] reading the brief and terribly rough notes which I took[40] at the staff meeting at the end of last month.[50] The items raised were so positive that I thought I[60] would definitely have no trouble at all recalling clearly but[70] I find that my memory is very defective and that[80] some of the points have now escaped me. I really[90] don't deserve any help but I observed your secretary, Daphne,[100] taking full notes and they are sure to be much[110] more effective than mine. Do you think she would be[120] kind enough to devote half an hour or so to[130] straightening out my tangled notes? D.C.

(137 words)

Typing Drill

(*a*)   I find that my memory is very defective.   8

(*b*)   They are sure to be much more effective than mine.   10

(*c*)   Do forgive me for bothering you for I know how busy you are.   12

Background Information Exercise — Pairs of words

Using your dictionary, look up the exact meanings of the following pairs of words. When you are sure that you know the difference between the words, type sentences to show their correct use:

defective	imperfect	definite	specific
stationary	stationery	unique	rare

Production — Memorandum

Use A5 paper turned sideways and insert today's date. Type in indented form.

Units 1-17

Short Form and Phrase Drill

with the ...., out of the ...., their ...., for whom ...., gentleman ....,

of man ...., in time ....

High Frequency Words

alone ...., world ...., start ...., court ....

Theory — Hooks 'n', 'f' and 'v' and the halving of finally hooked strokes

wind	....	bend	....	hand	....	round	....
Westland	....	around	....	England	....	second	....
mind	....	ascent	....	moment	....	friends	....
islands	....	blind	....	gift	....	rift	....

Reading — Book list

1 ....   10 ....

2 ....   11 ....

3 ....   12 ....

4 ....   13 ....

5 ....   14 ....

6 ....   15 ....

7 ....   16 ....

8 ....   17 ....

9 ....   18 ....

74

Dictation

1. Gone with the Wind
2. The Bend in the River
3. Left Hand, Right Hand
4. The Round Dozen
5. Out of the Westland
6. Sailing Alone Around the World
7. England, Their England
8. For Whom the Bell Tolls
9. Gentleman Jim
10. Second Start
11. Crime on Her Mind
12. The Ascent of Man
13. A Moment in Time
14. Friends at Court
15. Islands in the Sky
16. The Double Blind
17. The Gift of Love
18. The Rift in the Lute

Typing Drill

(*a*)	SAILING ALONE AROUND THE WORLD	6
(*b*)	T H E R O U N D D O Z E N	6
(*c*)	I S L A N D S I N T H E S K Y	7
(*d*)	T H E R I F T I N T H E L U T E	8

Background Information Exercise — 'Who' and 'whom'

Type the following sentences and insert 'who' or 'whom' as necessary:

(i)   The man . . . telephoned yesterday was an old friend of mine.
(ii)   The woman . . . you wished to see is absent today.
(iii)   The member of the Advisory Committee . . . we recently elected has now resigned.
(iv)   . . . shall we say is calling?

Production — Book list

Type on A5 paper. Using spaced capitals and double spacing, type the book list in alphabetical order with each item centred on the page. (The order of words in each title is to be exactly preserved.)

Units 1-17

Short Form and Phrase Drill

will be .... , very .... , rather than .... , from the .... , to hear .... ,

in some .... , of us .... , and I shall be .... , at the time .... , please let me

know .... , at once ....

High Frequency Words

urgent .... , calling .... , meeting .... , special .... , personally .... ,

importance .... , arrival .... , impossible ....

Theory — Figures

  (i) In straightforward continuous matter use shorthand outlines for the following
numerals:

    1 ....   3 ....   4 ....   5 ....   6 ....   7 ....   9 ....   10 ....

    (*Note:* 2 and 8 are never written in shorthand)

  (ii) The twenty-four hour clock can be represented in two ways — in full figures or with
stroke 'n' to represent the 'hundred':

    1600 ....   16 ....

               or

    1800 ....   18 ....

  (iii) The date can be represented with, or without, the 'th':

    9 1977   9 1977

               or

    13 1977   13 1977

Reading — Memo

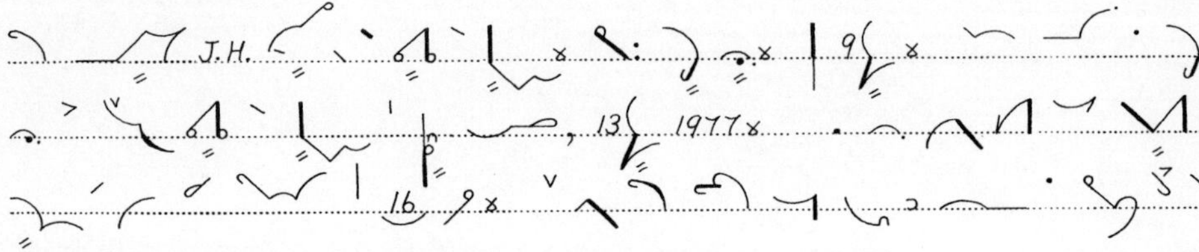

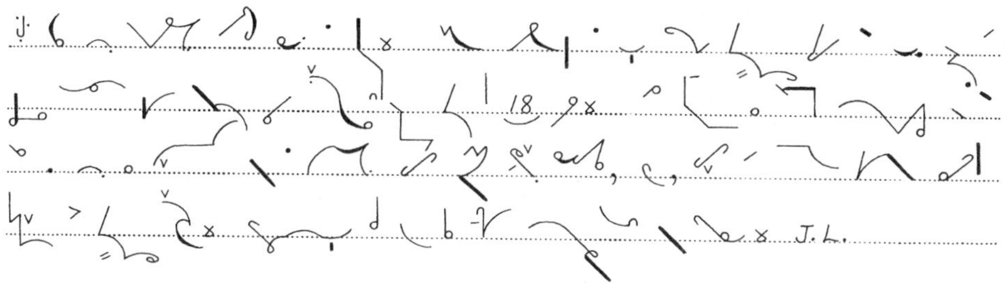

Dictation

From Colonel J. H. Lawrence to all Heads of Department.[10] Subject: Urgent Meeting. Date 9th July. I am calling an[20] urgent meeting of the five Heads of Department on Tuesday[30] next, 13th July 1977. The meeting will[40] be held in the Board Room and will start promptly[50] at 1600 hours. I should be very grateful indeed[60] if you would make a special point of attending this[70] meeting personally rather than sending a deputy. I have received[80] a note from the Chairman which we all need to[90] hear and discuss in some detail before he arrives to[100] take the chair at 1800 hours. As the topic[110] is of great importance to all of us the meeting[120] is likely to be a lengthy one and I shall[130] be supplying sandwiches, fruit, wine and coffee which will be[140] served at the time of the Chairman's arrival. Please let[150] me know at once if it is utterly impossible for[160] you to be present. J.L.

(166 words)

Typing Drill

(*a*) I have received a note from the Chairman.   8

(*b*) The meeting will be held in the Board Room and will start promptly at
1600 hours.   16

(*c*) As the topic is of great importance to all of us the meeting is likely to be a
lengthy one.   18

Background Information Exercise — Meetings

Type the following list of terms used in connection with meetings and type the meaning beside each:

(i)   minutes;
(ii) sub-committee;
(iii) resolution;
(iv) co-opted member;
(v)   casting vote.

Production — Memorandum

Type on A5 paper and in blocked style. There is no need for carbon copies as the original will be photocopied.

Units 1-17

High Frequency Words

regular ______, excellent ______, magazine ______, major ______, sport ______,

unfortunately ______, wife ______, even ______, bigger ______, better ______,

until ______, own ______, practical ______, illustrated ______, carefully ______

Theory — Revision of short forms and phrases

Dear Sir ______	I have been ______	for some time ______	always been ______
and I feel ______	that there is no ______	does not ______	over the years ______
from ______	did not ______	we now ______	very ______
think ______	more ______	I wish ______	before ______
Yours faithfully ______			

Reading — Letter

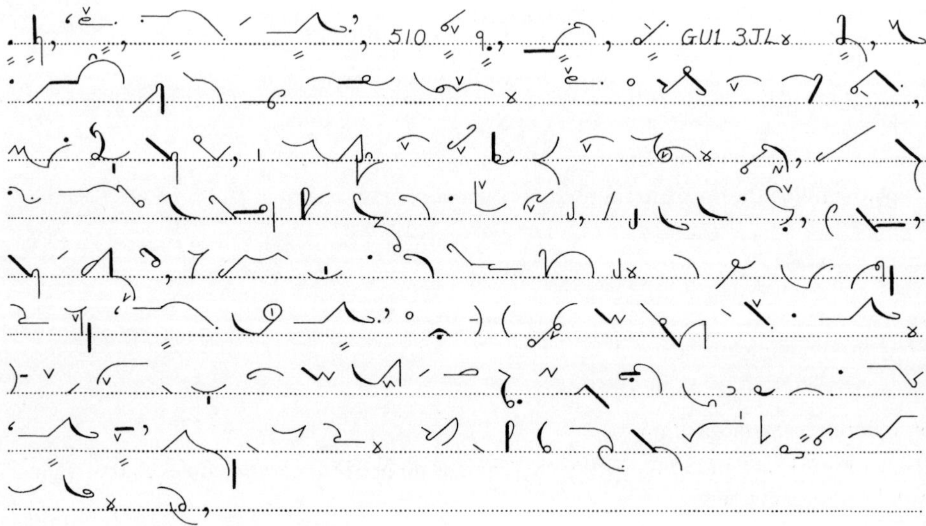

Dictation

The Editor, 'Cycling, Camping and Caravanning', 510 High[10] Street, Guildford, Surrey GU1 3JL. Dear[20] Sir, I have been a regular reader of your excellent[30] magazine for some time. Cycling has always been my major[40] hobby, and I feel that there is no better sport,[50] but unfortunately my wife does not share my enthusiasm. However,[60] we are both ardent campers and have progressed steadily over[70] the years from a tiny lightweight tent, which did not[80] even have a fly-sheet, through bigger, better and sturdier[90] brands, until we now own a very practical trailer tent.[100] Your recent fully illustrated article entitled 'Camping versus Caravanning' has[110] made us think seriously about the possibility of buying a[120] caravan. So I should like to know more about the[130] variety and cost of these and I should be grateful[140] if you would send me a copy of the 'Caravan[150] Guide' referred to in the article. I wish to study[160] this carefully before I look at the second-hand market[170] in vans. Yours faithfully,

(174 words)

Typing Drill

(*a*) I have been a regular reader of your excellent magazine for some time.   14

(*b*) I should be grateful if you would send me a copy of the 'Caravan Guide'.   15

(*c*) I wish to study this carefully before I look at the second-hand market in vans.

16

Background Information Exercise — Antonyms

By adding a prefix, give the opposite of each of the following words:

   regular   practical   possibility   grateful   voluntary   civil

Production — Letter

Use A5 paper. Put your home address and date the letter today. Type in fully-blocked style.

Units 1-17

High Frequency Words

summer ...., flat ...., work ...., however ...., important .... ,

opportunity ...., old ...., friends ...., through ....

Theory — Revision of phrases

for many years	part of the	last year	in spite of the
as soon as	it is not possible	for us	as we have been
business meetings	United States of America	we shall be able to	in New York
as we shall be	in this city	at least	we think you will agree
with us	that there is no	to let you know	that we hope
that you will be able to	other ar-rangements	so that we can	

Reading — Personal letter

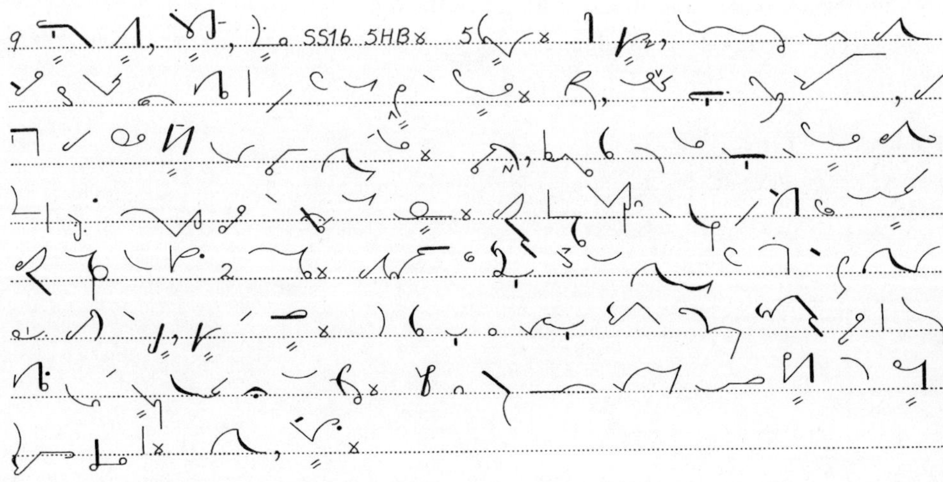

Dictation

9 Globe Road, Basildon, Essex SS16 5[10]HB. 5th April. Dear Gillian, For many years now[20] we have always spent part of the summer holidays at[30] our flat in the South of France. Last year, in[40] spite of the growing pressure of work, we got away[50] as soon as George felt he could leave the office.[60] However, it is not possible this year for us to[70] go to France as we have been asked to attend[80] an important series of business meetings in the United States[90] of America. We shall be able to take this opportunity[100] to visit our old friends in New York as we[110] shall be in this city for at least two months.[120] We think you will agree with us that there is[130] no point in leaving the flat empty all through the[140] lovely sunny weather of June, July and August. So this[150] note is to let you know that we hope very[160] much that you will be able to use it for[170] your holidays if you and Peter have not yet made[180] any other arrangements. I suggest you both come to lunch[190] next Saturday or Sunday so that we can discuss it.[200] Love, Pauline.

(202 words)

Typing Drill

(*a*) We hope very much that you will be able to use it. 10

(*b*) We have been asked to attend an important series of business meetings. 14

(*c*) We think you will agree with us that there is no point in leaving the flat empty. 16

Background Information Exercise — Line-end division

Three of the following words should not be split. Which are they? Type them first. Then type the other words and indicate the division with a hyphen:

Basildon   summer   holidays   America   opportunity   lovely arrangements   discuss

Production — Personal letter

Type on A4 paper leaving a wide left-hand margin. Use indented style and put Gillian's address at the bottom left-hand corner as follows: Mrs G. Ripon, 'Sandilands', 4 Grange Court, Peterborough PE3 6PD.

Units 1-17

High Frequency Words

remember .... , rare .... , never .... , during .... , August .... ,

October ....

Theory — Revision of phrases and intersections

do you	some months ago	we arranged	to meet ....
on one	of my	every time	at last ....
I think arrangements	be made	for us	three times ....
three months	I shall be	next month	some arrangements ....
can be made	as early as possible		

Reading — Personal letter

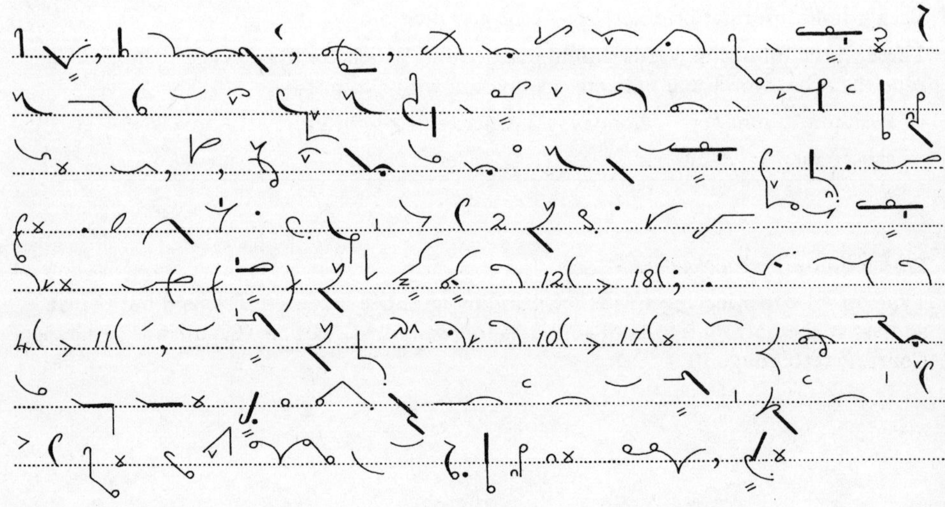

Assignment 39

Dictation

Dear Bill, Do you remember that, some months ago, we[10] arranged to meet on one of my rare trips to[20] Glasgow? Although I have kept this in mind every time[30] I have travelled to Scotland I never seem to coincide[40] with dates suitable for you. Now, at last, I think[50] arrangements might be made for us to meet as I[60] have to be in Glasgow three times during the next[70] three months. The first will be only a fleeting visit[80] but for the other two I shall be spending a[90] whole week in the Glasgow area. Next month (August) I[100] shall be at the Royal Hotel from 12th to the[110] 18th; the following month from 4th to the 11th and,[120] in October I shall be touring around the area from[130] 10th to the 17th. I am sure some arrangements can[140] be made for us to get together. Jean is hoping[150] to be able to come with me in October but[160] she will not be with me on either of the[170] other trips. Please write as early as possible if any[180] of these dates suit you. Sincerely, Geoffrey.

(187 words)

Typing Drill

(a)	I think arrangements might be made for us to meet.	10
(b)	I shall be touring around the area from 10th to the 17th.	12
(c)	I have to be in Glasgow three times in the next three months.	12
(d)	Please write as early as possible if any of these dates suit you.	13

Background Information Exercise — Pairs of words

Using your dictionary, look up the exact meanings of the following pairs of words. When you are sure that you know the difference between the words, type sentences to show their correct use:

coincide	synchronize	prosecute	persecute
recent	modern	appreciate	understand

Production — Personal letter

Use A5 paper. Put your home address and date the letter for some time in July. Type in indented style.

Units 1-17

Short Form and Phrase Drill

Dear Mr ...., very much ...., yesterday ...., of course ...., to go ...., to us ...., without delay ...., will have ...., their ...., and send you ...., we think you will find ...., look forward ...., yours sincerely ....

High Frequency Words

telephone ...., members ...., carefully ...., throughout ...., journey ...., reasonable ...., world ....

Theory — Intersections

Supplies Company		to make	Sales Department	next month
standard form		our	and we will arrange	our charges
more business		business		

Reading — Letter

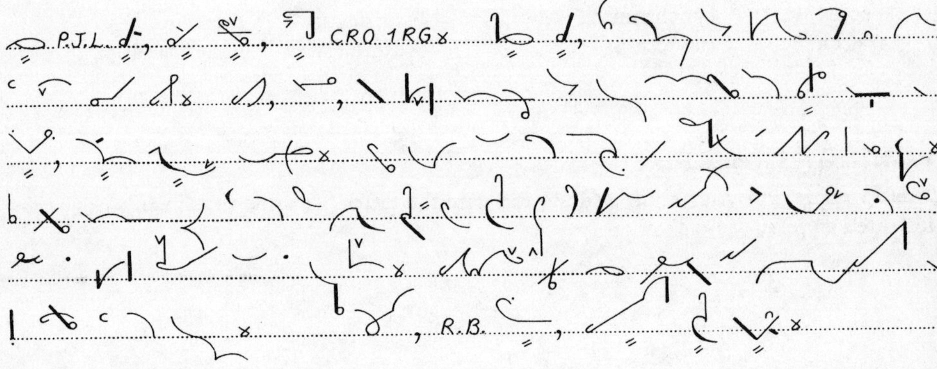

Dictation

Mr P. J. L. Jones, Surrey Supplies Company, Croydon C[10] R0 1RG. Dear Mr Jones, Thank you[20] very much for the telephone message you left with my[30] secretary yesterday. We shall, of course, be delighted to make[40] arrangements for the four members of your Sales Department to[50] go to Paris, Rome and Vienna next month. Please fill[60] in very carefully our standard form and return it to[70] us without delay. It is our business to make sure[80] that your staff will have trouble-free travel throughout their[90] journey and we will arrange all the various air flights[100] and send you a detailed itinerary in a few days[110] time. We think you will find our charges most reasonable[120] and we look forward to doing more business with your[130] firm. Yours sincerely, R. B. Flack, World Travel Bureau.

(139 words)

Typing Drill

(*a*) Thank you very much for the telephone message.   9

(*b*) We shall, of course, be delighted to make arrangements.   11

(*c*) We look forward to doing more business with your firm.   11

Background Information Exercise — Abbreviations

Can you give the full-length form for the following abbreviations? Type in one list, in alphabetical order, and add the full form beside each one:

COY   IE   SS   CIF   INC   ENC   SAE

MA   DSO   MP

Production — Letter

Type on A5 paper, in fully-blocked style, and date the letter today. Take a carbon copy.

Units 1-21

Short Form and Phrase Drill

Pharmaceutical Co Ltd .... , in view .... , trade .... , it has been .... ,

will take charge .... , businessmen .... , who have been .... , for many

years .... , with them .... , satisfactorily .... , instead of .... ,

in future .... , at one .... , may we take .... , you have .... ,

always .... , Yours faithfully ....

High Frequency Words

pleasure .... , great .... , increase .... , Manager .... , inquiries .... ,

opportunity ....

Theory — Double-length curved strokes

Curved strokes are doubled in length to represent the sounds of 'ter', 'der', 'ther',
'THer' and 'ture'. Circle 's' may be added to these double-length strokes, as may hook
'n':

Walter ....   Easterbrook ....   Lavender ....   Netherton ....

Featherstone ....   Sunderland ....   Anderson ....   Porter ....

orders ....

Reading — Circular letter

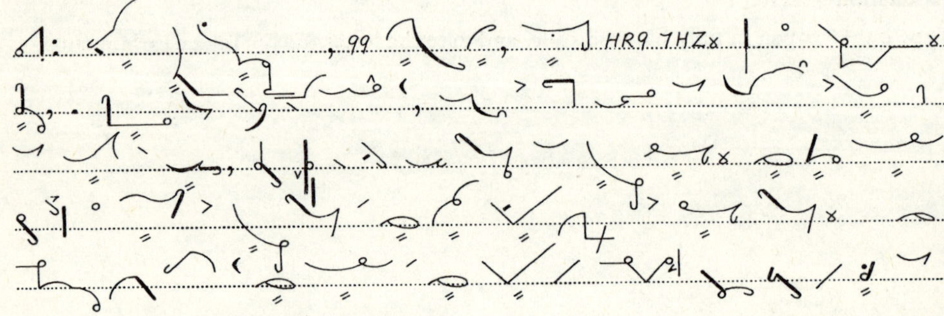

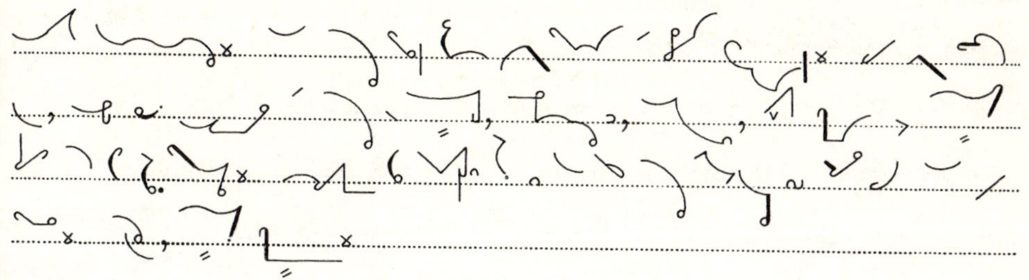

Dictation

Heading: Walter Easterbrook Pharmaceutical Co Ltd, 99 Lavender Lane,[10] Netherton HR9 7HZ. Date as postmark.[20] Dear Sirs, The Directors have the pleasure to announce that,[30] in view of the great increase in the volume of[40] the Company's trade in the North of England, it has[50] been decided to open new branches in Featherstone and Sunderland.[60] Mr James Anderson has been appointed as Manager of the[70] Featherstone branch and Mr Leslie Porter will take charge of[80] the Sunderland branch. Most customers will be aware that Mr[90] Anderson and Mr Porter are experienced businessmen who have been[100] our Agents in the north for many years. Any orders[110] placed with them will be promptly and satisfactorily fulfilled. We[120] should be grateful if, instead of sending inquiries and orders[130] to Netherton, customers would, in future, write directly to the[140] Manager at one or other of these branches. May we[150] take this opportunity of thanking you for past orders and[160] for the confidence you have always shown in our products.[170] Yours faithfully, Managing Director.

(174 words)

Typing Drill

(a) It has been decided to open new branches.   8

(b) Mr James Anderson has been appointed as Manager.   10

(c) May we take this opportunity of thanking you for past orders.   12

Background Information Exercise — Pairs of words

Using your dictionary, look up the meanings of the following pairs of words. When you are sure that you know the difference between the words, type sentences to show their correct use:

announce	assert	confidence	trust
strange	bizarre	necessary	essential

Production — Circular letter

Type the letter on A4 paper. Centre the firm's name and address on the page. Leave sufficient space for any addressee to be inserted later. Type in indented style and leave room for the Managing Director's signature.

Units 1-21

Short Form and Phrase Drill

Dear Louis .... , I have been .... , what has .... , your letter .... ,

in Rome .... , this month .... , I was .... , very pleased .... , I will be

there .... , I think there is .... , will be .... , I have been there ....

High Frequency Words

posted .... , telegram .... , morning .... , why ....

Theory — Double-length straight strokes

Straight strokes are doubled in length to represent the sounds of 'ter', 'der', 'ther', 'THer' and 'ture' when they follow another stroke, or when they are finally hooked:

Hunter ....   Canterbury ....   Winter-bourne ....   wondering ....

winter ....   Doctor ....   Painter ....   Investigator ....

character ....   further ....   Anstruther ....   Director ....

Panther ....

Reading — Personal letter

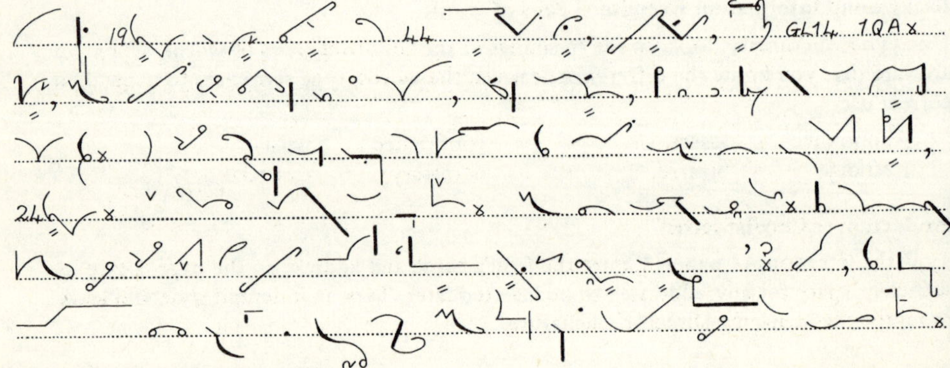

88

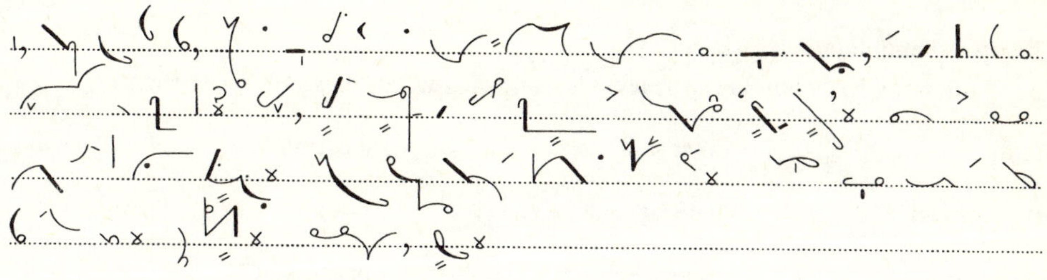

Dictation

Letter dated 19th April to Louis Hunter from 44[10] Canterbury Lane, Winterbourne, Gloucestershire GL14 1Q[20]A. Dear Louis, I have been wondering what has happened[30] to you as your letter, posted in Rome, said you[40] would definitely be in London early this month. So I[50] was very pleased indeed to get your telegram this morning[60] inviting me to your party on Saturday, 24th April.[70] I promise I will be there in good time. I[80] have some incredible news for you. Do you remember the[90] television series I was writing last winter called 'Doctor Painter[100] — Supreme Investigator'? Well, this detective character seems to have caught[110] the viewers' imagination and I have been asked to do[120] a further series for next autumn. But, better even than[130] this, I think there is a good chance that a[140] full-length film is going to be made, and who[150] do you think is likely to direct it? Why, John[160] Anstruther who was the Director of the fabulous 'Blue Panther'.[170] Some of the scenes will be shot at Lake Geneva.[180] I have been there several times before and it will[190] be an ideal spot. I must close now and post[200] this off to you. See you on Saturday. Sincerely, Stephen.[210]

(210 words)

Typing Drill

(*a*) I promise I will be there in good time. 8

(*b*) Do you remember the television series I was writing last winter? 13

(*c*) I think there is a good chance that a full-length film is going to be made. 15

Background Information Exercise — Pairs of words

Using your dictionary, look up the meanings of the following pairs of words. When you are sure that you know the difference between the words, type sentences to show their correct use:

incredible	incredulous	historic	historical
consigned	assigned	audience	congregation

Production — Personal letter

Type on A4 paper leaving a wide left-hand margin. Use indented style.

Units 1-21

Theory — 'shun' hook

The 'shun' hook has a number of rules. The following words illustrate six of them:

nation	mansion	location
international	educational	national
professional	television	permission
functions	situation	additional
technician	decision	instructions

Decide which words fit each of the following rules. Make a list of the words and their outlines and state the number of the rule which applies to each:

Rule 1. 'Shun' hook is written inside curves.

Rule 2. 'Shun' hook is written on the opposite side to an initial circle or hook to balance the outline.

Rule 3. 'Shun' hook is written on the opposite side to the preceding vowel sound.

Rule 4. 'Shun' hook is written on the right-hand side of simple 't', 'd' or 'j'.

Rule 5. After _______________________________ the 'shun' hook is written away from the curve to balance the outline.

Rule 6. When 'shun' follows the 's', 'z' or 'ns', 'nz' circle it is represented by a small hook written opposite the circle.

Reading — Telegram

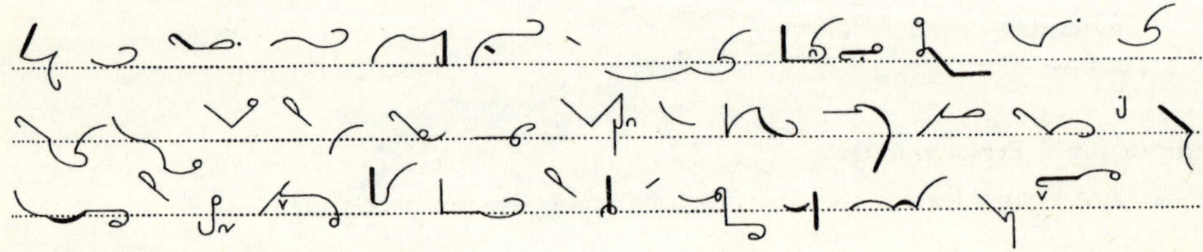

Dictation

```
JONATHAN    NATION            FOR     TELEVISION    COVERAGE
BROADCASTING    MANSION       REQUEST    PERMISSION    ATTEND
LONDON    LOCATION    OF      BOTH    FUNCTIONS    STOP 30
INTERNATIONAL    EDUCATIONAL  SITUATION    REQUIRES
CONGRESS 10    STRASBOURG     ADDITIONAL    TECHNICIAN
FOLLOWING    NATIONAL         STOP    DECISION    AND
PROFESSIONAL    CONFERENCE    INSTRUCTIONS    NEEDED
PARIS    STOP    WILL    PRESENT    IMMEDIATELY 40    PETER    GRIMES
EXCELLENT 20    OPPORTUNITY
```

(42 words)

Typing Drill

(*a*) Please send me instructions immediately.   8

(*b*) I need permission to attend both these functions.   10

(*c*) The International Educational Congress will be held in Strasbourg.   14

(*d*) This will present us with an excellent opportunity for television coverage.   15

Background Information Exercise — Typing telegrams

Telegrams are typed in block capitals with three or four spaces between words. The meaning must be clear without the aid of any punctuation, but the word 'stop' may be inserted to indicate the end of a sentence where there might otherwise be confusion.

Compose and type a telegram on the occasion of the wedding of a member of the office staff, from her colleagues.

Production — Telegram

Type the telegram from Peter Grimes using A5 paper turned sideways (or on a telegram form if you have one). Type in block capitals with three spaces between the words. Type the initial name and address on a separate line. Take a carbon copy.

Units 1-21

Short Form and Phrase Drill

other day .... , to the Continent .... , sixth form .... , I was .... ,
my attention .... , I felt .... , European Communities .... ,
first-class .... , by the Commission .... , range of .... , information .... ,
you will find ....

High Frequency Words

when .... , future .... , students .... , publications .... , school .... ,
children .... , gives .... , Common .... , Market .... , picture .... ,
Council .... , individual ....

Theory — 'shun' hook

mentioned ....   vacation ....   introduction ....   institutions ....
illustrations ....   foundations ....   section ....   affectionately ....

Reading — Personal letter

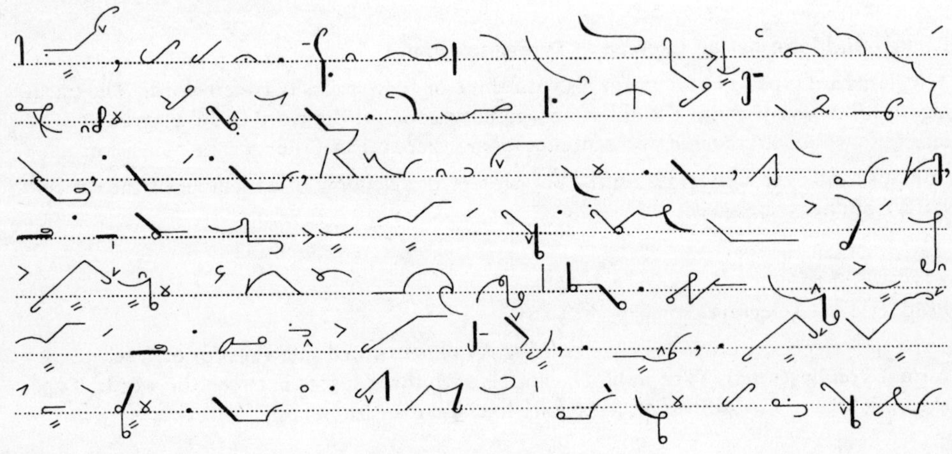

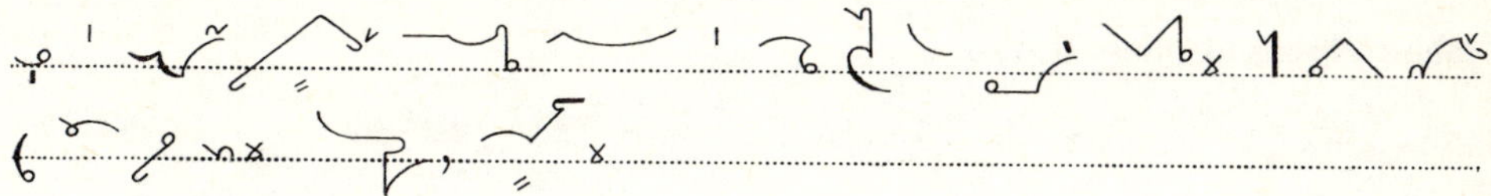

Dictation

Dear Caroline, When we met the other day you mentioned[10] your future vacation trip to the Continent with some of[20] your fifth and sixth form students. I was browsing in[30] the bookshop the very next day and my attention was[40] drawn to two excellent publications, a book and a booklet,[50] which I felt you would like to have. The book,[60] written for school children, gives a good basic introduction to[70] the Common Market and provides a comprehensive picture of the[80] origins and institutions of the European Communities. With the help[90] of some colourful illustrations it describes the historical foundations of[100] the Common Market and gives a first-class account of[110] the work done by the Commission, the Council, the European[120] Parliament and the Court of Justice. The booklet has a[130] wide range of information on school visits. One section provides[140] useful notes on individual European countries and another on methods[150] of travel for school parties. I do hope you will[160] find these of some use to you. Affectionately, Margaret.

(169 words)

Typing Drill

(*a*) You mentioned your vacation trip to the Continent. 10

(*b*) One section provides useful notes on individual European countries. 13

(*c*) The book, written for school children, gives a good basic introduction to the Common Market. 18

Background Information Exercise — Currencies

Make a list, in alphabetical order, of the following eight countries:

Spain, France, Austria, Denmark, Italy, Canada, Netherlands, Portugal.

List also the currency used in each country.

Production — Personal letter

Use A5 paper. Put your own home address and today's date. Type in indented form.

Units 1-21

Short Form and Phrase Drill

New York ...., he has ...., several ...., very ...., difficult .... ,

almost ...., not only ...., altogether ...., unsatisfactory .... , some

completely ...., but this is ...., out of ...., more ...., there must .... ,

which have ...., I cannot ...., I can ...., that you could ....

High Frequency Words

Doctor ...., investigation ...., impossible ...., problems ....,

solutions ...., him ...., character ...., matter ...., grateful ....

Theory — Negative words

The strokes 'm', 'n' and upward 'l' are repeated to form the negatives in outlines beginning with 'm', 'n' or upward 'l':

unnecessary ....   illogical ....   unnoticed ....

The negative of an outline beginning with upward 'r' is written with a downward 'r' in front of the upward 'r' stroke:

irrelevant ....

Other negative words are written:

unreliable ....   unlike ....   inconsistent ....   unfortunately ....

undisturbed ....   independent ....

Reading — Memo

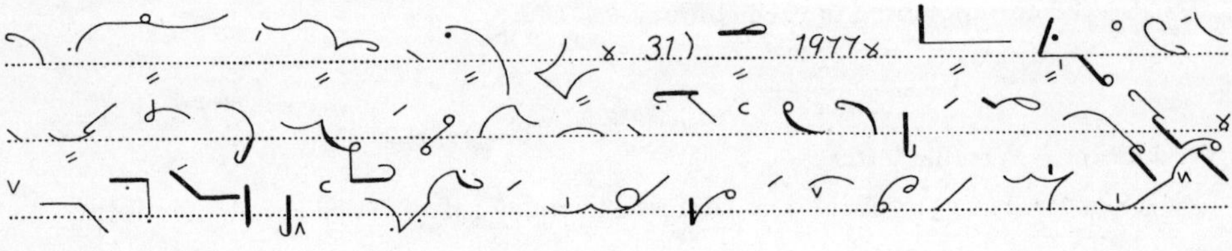

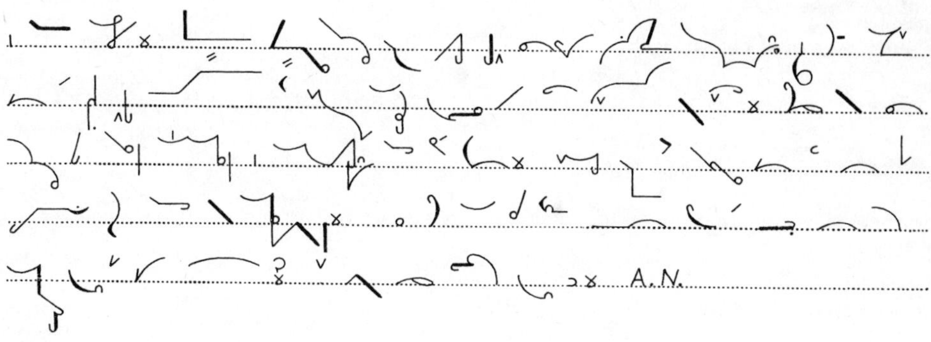

Dictation

From Alexander Norman to Arthur Shipley. 31st August 1977.[10] Dr Jacobs has flown off to New York[20] on some urgent investigation and he has left me to[30] grapple with several very difficult and almost impossible problems. I[40] keep getting bogged down with irrelevant and unnecessary detaiis and[50] my solutions are not only unreliable but altogether unsatisfactory. Dr[60] Jacobs appears to have written down some completely illogical formulae[70] but this is so unlike him and totally out of[80] character that I fear the inconsistent figures are more likely[90] to be mine. There must be some errors which have[100] passed unnoticed but unfortunately I cannot spot them. I intend[110] to take all the papers home with me at the[120] weekend so that I can be undisturbed. Is there any[130] chance that you could come over and give me your[140] independent view on the whole matter? I should be most[150] grateful if you would. A.N.

(156 words)

Typing Drill

(*a*)	I intend to take all the papers home with me.	9
(*b*)	There must be some errors which have passed unnoticed.	11
(*c*)	Dr Jacobs has flown off to New York on some urgent investigation.	14

Background Information Exercise — Plurals

Type the following words in a list and beside each give the plural form:

formula, memorandum, agenda, son-in-law, woman, court-martial

Production — Memorandum

Type on A5 paper, in blocked style.

Units 1-21

Short Form and Phrase Drill

I was .... , your letter .... , I can .... , information .... , in fact .... ,

very much .... , first-class .... , he was .... , I think there is .... ,

if there is .... , anything .... , why not ....

High Frequency Words

interested .... , distinguished .... , career .... , school .... , college .... ,

recognised .... , university .... , never .... , quite ....

Theory — Suffix 'ship'
The suffix 'ship' is written as a joined or disjoined 'sh':

friendship ....   Lordship ....   Ladyship ....   scholarship ....

headship ....   principal-ship ....   leadership ....   chairman-ship ....

censorship ....   professor-ship ....   relationship ....

Reading — Personal letter

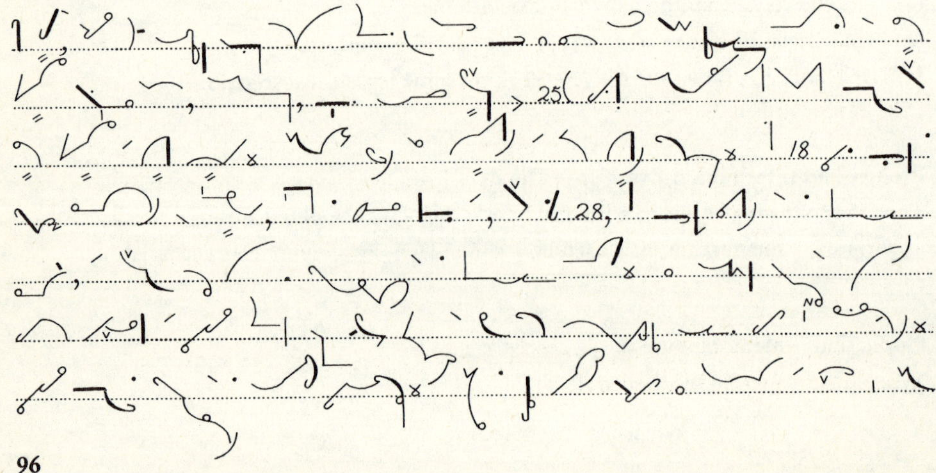

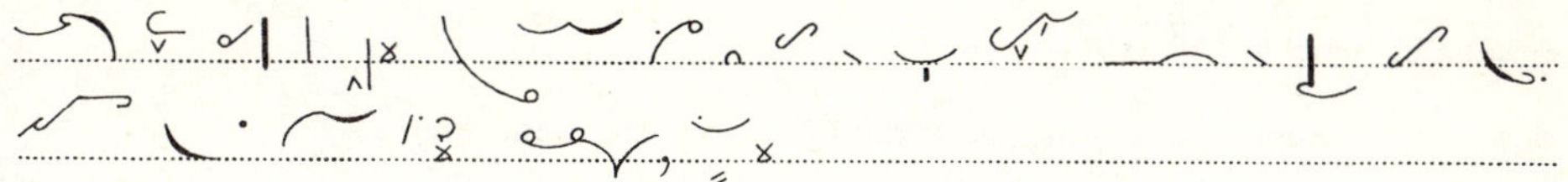

Dictation

Dear John, I was so interested to get your letter[10] asking if I can give you some information about the[20] distinguished career of Sir Charles because I am, in fact,[30] going next Friday to the twenty-fifth wedding anniversary party[40] given by Sir Charles and Lady Mary. I value the[50] friendship of his Lordship and her Ladyship very much. At[60] 18 he gained a brilliant scholarship to Oxford, got a[70] first-class degree and, by the age of 28,[80] had gained the headship of a technical school, and five[90] years later the principal-ship of a technical college. His undoubted[100] powers of leadership were recognised and he was asked to[110] take over the chairman-ship of several very important committees including[120] one on censorship. He was given a professorship of a[130] northern university. I think there is a distant relationship between[140] his family and mine but I have never quite sorted[150] it out. If there is anything else you want to[160] know why not come to dinner one evening and we[170] can have a long chat? Sincerely, Anne.

(177 words)

Typing Drill

(*a*)   I was so interested to get your letter.   8

(*b*)   At 18 he gained a brilliant scholarship to Oxford.   10

(*c*)   His undoubted powers of leadership were recognised.   10

Background Information Exercise — Line-end division

Type the following words and indicate where the best line-end division could occur:

information, anniversary, wedding, scholarship, school, recognized, university, distant

Production — Personal letter

Type on A5 paper. Put your own home address at the top right-hand corner and date the letter today. Type in indented form.

Units 1-21

Short Form and Phrase Drill

city requirements .... , junior required .... , busy Department .... ,
by arrangement .... , large company .... , well-known .... , Personnel
Department .... , city company .... , could ....

High Frequency Words

secretary .... , translation .... , mother .... , English .... , either .... ,
senior .... , London ....

Theory — 'kw' and 'gw'

A large hook added to 'k' and 'g' represents the sounds of 'kw' and 'gw'. Circle 's' is
written inside the hook:

quick .... bi-lingual .... language .... required ....

quite .... frequent .... well- .... enquiries ....
qualified

square ....

Reading — Notice of appointments

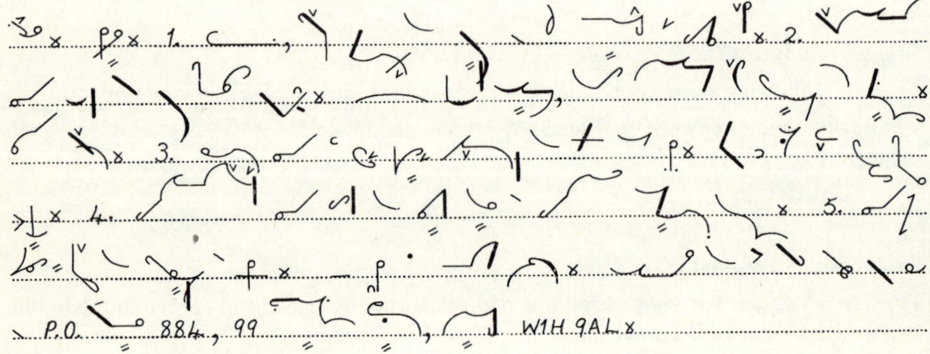

Dictation

Appointments. City Requirements. 1. Quick, bright junior required for busy[10] Department to assist Accountant on the wages side. 2. Bi-[20]lingual secretary needed by busy translation bureau. Mother tongue English,[30] foreign language either French or German. Salary by arrangement. 3.[40] Senior secretary with fluent Italian required for large company in[50] the city. Job would entail quite frequent trips to the[60] Continent. 4. Well-qualified secretary wanted for Head Office of[70] well-known Engineering firm. 5. Secretary/shorthand-typist for Personnel[80] Department of city company. Could suit a college leaver. Enquiries[90] for all the above positions to be sent to P.[100]O. Box 884, 99 Grantham Square, London[110] W1H 9AL.

(116 words)

Typing Drill

(a) A quick, bright junior is required. 7

(b) A bi-lingual secretary is needed by busy translation bureau. 12

(c) The job would entail quite frequent trips to the Continent. 12

Background Information Exercise — Hyphens

Type a copy of the following:

No two dictionaries seem to give exactly the same advice regarding the correct use of the hyphen.

However, the main function of a hyphen is to indicate that two or more words are meant to be read together as a single word with its own meaning.

Over six paragraphs are devoted to this subject in the reference book, *Fowler's Modern English Usage*, revised by Sir Ernest Gowers.

Production — Notice of appointments

On A5 paper, type the list of appointments. Type the word 'Appointments' in spaced capitals, 'City Requirements' in capital letters and the list of five appointments in single spacing, in blocked form and with three spaces between each item.

Units 1-21

Short Form and Phrase Drill

I went .... , wonderful concert .... , I thought .... , he said .... , it would be .... ,

difficult .... , before the .... , with us ....

High Frequency Words

house .... , during .... , interval .... , unexpectedly .... ,

younger .... , brother .... , surprised .... , him .... , December .... ,

January ....

Theory — 'wh'
The sound of 'wh' is represented by .... :

Wheeler .... White .... Whitley Bay .... somewhere ....

while .... whether .... what .... when ....

why ....

Reading — Personal letter

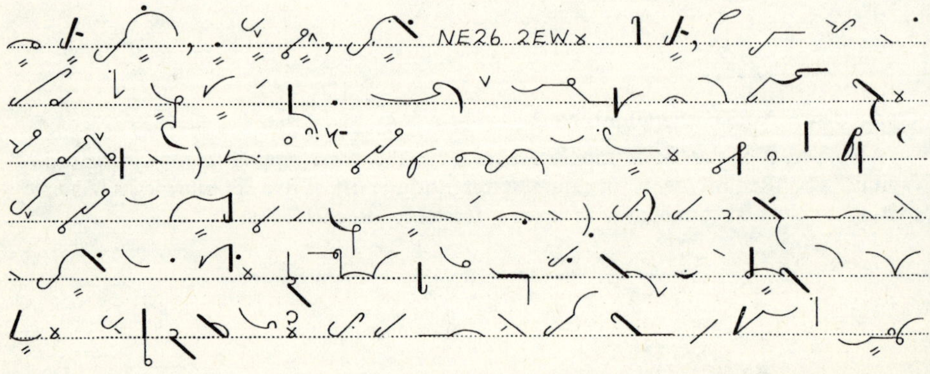

Dictation

Miss Joan Wheeler, The White House, Whitley Bay NE[10]26 2EW. Dear Joan, Last week I[20] went to a wonderful concert at the Festival Hall and[30] during the interval I unexpectedly met your younger brother. I[40] was surprised to see him as I thought he was[50] still somewhere in Africa. He said you had suggested that[60] while he was in London he should visit Mother and[70] me to see whether we would both come up to[80] Whitley Bay for a holiday. It would be extremely difficult[90] for us to get away before the end of December[100] or early January. What dates would be best for you?[110] When we come up we will break our journey at[120] Newcastle to visit my aunt and uncle. Why don't you[130] all think about coming to London to spend Christmas with[140] us? With love, Virginia.

(144 words)

Typing Drill

(*a*) I thought he was still somewhere in Africa. 9

(*b*) When we come up we will break our journey at Newcastle. 11

(*c*) Last week I went to a wonderful concert at the Festival Hall. 13

Background Information Exercise — Counties

In which counties would you find the following? Check in an atlas:

Whitley Bay, Luton, Leatherhead, Doncaster, Crewe, Lampeter, Bristol, Bridlington, Salisbury.

Type a list in alphabetical order of counties.

Production — Personal letter

Type on A5 paper and in blocked style. Put your own address in the top right-hand corner and date the letter 8th December.

Units 1-21

Short Form and Phrase Drill

I want .... , Company's Board .... , who have .... , that they are considering .... ,

International Congress .... , in New York .... , next month .... ,

from .... , do not .... , should be glad .... , immediate confirmation .... ,

at the end .... , already been .... , of this city .... , as soon as possible .... ,

to be able to contact .... , Travel Department .... , travel arrangements .... ,

I think you will agree contains .... , any comments ....

High Frequency Words

members .... , number .... , paragraph .... , distribution .... ,

intention .... , accommodation .... , detailed .... , important ....

Theory — Dot 'con' and 'com'

The sounds 'con' and 'com' at the *beginning* of a word are represented by a dot written at
the beginning of the first stroke in the outline. The position of the outline is determined
by the first vowel sound *following* 'con' or 'com':

considering .... Congress .... completely .... Connaught ....

Consett .... Conway .... confirmation .... confirm ....

contact .... complete .... conference .... contains ....

Reading — Memo

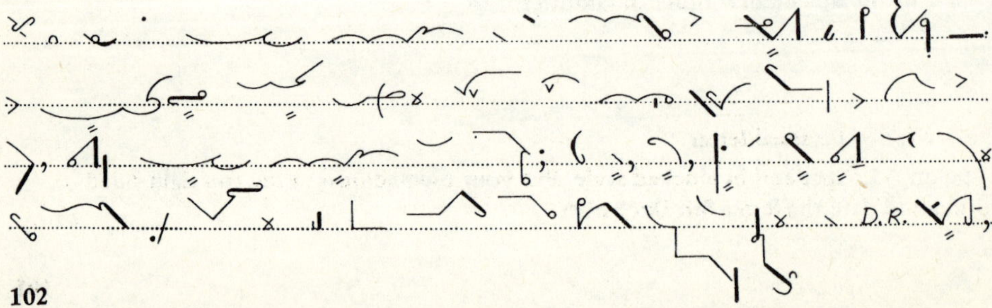

Dictation

I want you to send an internal memorandum to all[10] members of the Company's Board who have said that they[20] are considering going to the International Congress in New York[30] next month. I like my memos to be completely blocked[40] to the left of the page, headed INTERNAL MEMORANDUM in[50] capitals; then TO, FROM, DATE and SUBJECT headings in that[60] order. Please number each paragraph. Do not take carbon copies[70] as it will be photocopied for distribution. To D. R.[80] Bolton, P. J. Connaught, E. L. Consett (two t's), D.[90] J. Conway, S. B. Lund. 1. I should be glad[100] to have immediate confirmation of your intention to attend the[110] Congress in New York at the end of next month.[120] 2. Provisional hotel accommodation has already been booked in the[130] centre of this city and I should like to confirm[140] the booking as soon as possible. 3. I should also[150] like to be able to contact the Travel Department to[160] ask them to complete the travel arrangements for our flight[170] on 28th May. 4. I am attaching the detailed[180] Conference programme which I think you will agree contains many[190] important items. 5. I shall be interested to have any[200] comments you may wish to make.

(206 words)

Typing Drill

(*a*) I am attaching the detailed Conference programme. 10

(*b*) Provisional hotel accommodation has already been booked. 11

Background Information Exercise — Spelling

'Accommodation' is one of the words most commonly mis-spelt. Here are some other words which often cause difficulty. Type a correct list in alphabetical order:

> sieze, refered, embarass, committee, arguement, acreage, comparitively, carefull.

Production — Memorandum

Type on A4 paper. Memo has been dictated by L. A. Janes and should be dated 26th April. Subject heading is 'International Congress'. Put a reference consisting of the initials of the dictator followed by your own.

Units 1-21

Short Form and Phrase Drill

Dear Sirs ...., to learn ...., from your letter ...., this is the ...., of this nature ...., that we have ever ...., to hear ...., that this may ...., Despatch Department ...., this matter ...., Yours faithfully ....

High Frequency Words

order ...., delivered ...., against ...., rather ...., structure ...., however ...., urgently ...., requested ...., swiftly ....

Theory — 'con' and 'com'

Constable ....   Congrieve ....   Construction ....   Common ....

Condover ....   consignment ....   complaint ....   condition ....

In the middle of an outline 'con', 'com', 'cum' or 'cog' is represented by writing the stroke following any of these sounds close to the preceding stroke and omitting the dot:

inconvenience ....

In phrases the dot 'con' or 'com' is omitted and the sound of 'con' or 'com' is expressed by writing outlines close together:

Congrieve Construction Company ....   first complaint ....

of our containers ....   perfect condition ....

Reading — Letter

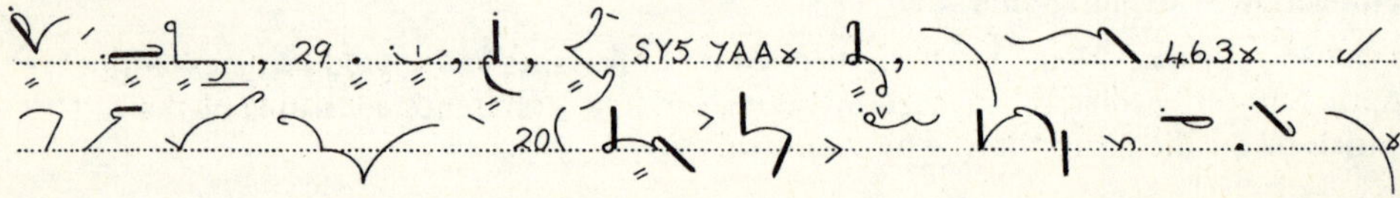

"""

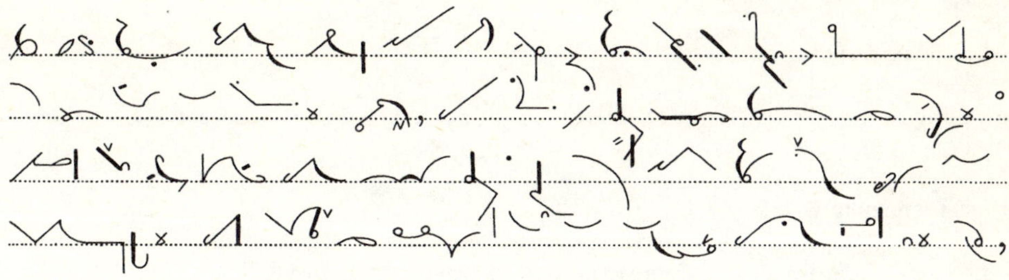

Dictation

Constable & Congrieve Construction Company, 29 The Common, Condover,[10] Shropshire SY5 7AA. Dear Sirs, Order[20] number 463. We much regret to learn from[30] your letter of 20th December of the damage to the[40] consignment delivered to you against the above order. This is[50] the first complaint of this nature that we have ever[60] received and we are rather upset to hear that this[70] may possibly be attributable to the structure of our containers[80] or to some fault in packing. However, we are asking[90] our Despatch Department to examine this matter most urgently. As[100] requested by you over the telephone we have immediately despatched[110] a duplicate order and we hope that this will arrive[120] swiftly and in perfect condition. We do apologise most sincerely[130] for any inconvenience we may have caused you. Yours faithfully,[140]

(140 words)

Typing Drill

(*a*) We have immediately despatched a duplicate order.   10

(*b*) We are asking our Despatch Department to examine this matter.   13

(*c*) This is the first complaint of this nature that we have ever received.   14

Background Information Exercise — Spelling

The following words all end in 'able' or 'ible'. Type the complete words in a single list:

attribut . . . .   contempt . . . .   suscept . . . .   penetr . . . .   indel . . . .

perish . . . .   notice . . . .   imposs . . . .   tang . . . .

Production — Letter

Type the letter on A4 paper. Leave sufficient space for a printed heading. Date the letter the 22nd December and mark it for the attention of Mr J. R. Foster. Type in fully-blocked style and leave a wide left-hand margin.

Units 1-21

Short Form Drill

anything ...., trade ...., particularly ...., nevertheless ...., several ....

High Frequency Words

much ...., rather ...., figures ...., improve ...., future ....,

publicity ...., return ...., products ...., foreign ....

Theory — Revision of phrases

I know there is	very little	state of affairs	I am confident
and that we shall continue	for your consideration	very glad	as quickly as possible
without delay	in any case	later than the	of some other ways
immediate attention	many thanks		

Reading — Memo

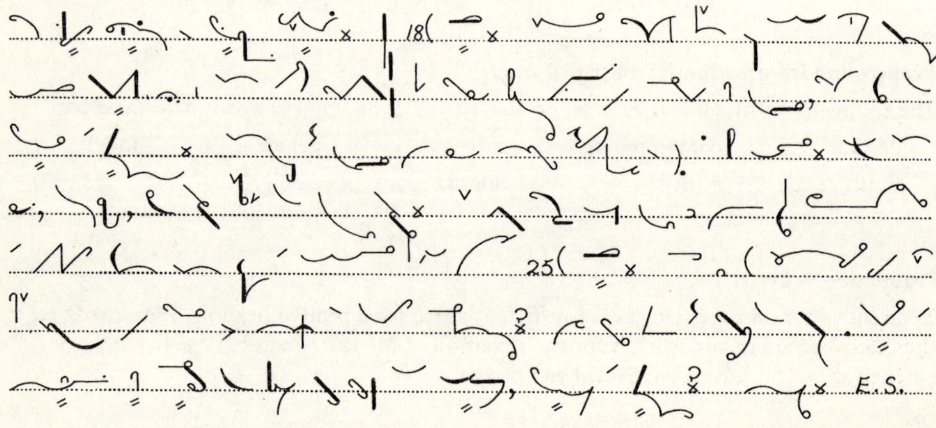

Assignment 51

Dictation

From Edwin Seymour to Frederick Whitefield. Dated 18th August. I[10] know there is very little time to do anything much[20] before the next Board meeting but I am rather perturbed[30] at the present state of affairs regarding our export trade[40] figures, particularly those for France and Germany. I am confident[50] that the figures will soon improve and that we shall[60] continue to see a steady increase. Nevertheless I am sending,[70] for your consideration, several possible ideas for future publicity. I[80] should be very glad indeed if you would look at[90] these as quickly as possible and return them to me[100] without delay and in any case not later than the[110] 25th August. Can you think of some other ways[120] we might try to bring our products to the immediate[130] attention of foreign customers? Will you please check that the[140] brochures for both the Paris and Munich Trade Exhibitions have[150] definitely been printed in English, French and German? Many thanks.[160] E.S.

(162 words)

Typing Drill

(*a*) I am confident that the figures will soon improve.   10

(*b*) I should be very glad indeed if you would look at these.   11

(*c*) I know there is very little time to do anything much before the next Board meeting.   17

Background Information Exercise — Pairs of words

Using your dictionary, look up the exact meanings of the following pairs of words. When you are sure that you know the difference between the words, type sentences to show their correct use:

perturbed	disturbed	confident	confidant
increase	expand	delay	defer

Production — Memorandum

Type on A5 paper and in blocked style. Take a carbon copy.

Units 1-21

High Frequency Words

from .... , travel .... , received .... , appointment .... , export .... ,

manager .... , interviews .... , middle .... , absence ....

Theory — Revision of intersections

arrange/arranged/arrangement	make arrangements	
attention	personal attention	
business	international business	
charge	take charge	
company	company headquarters	
company limited	paper company limited	
corporation	large corporation	
department	my department	
form	application forms	
enquire/enquiry	urgent enquiry	
month	next month	
require/required/requirement	situation requires	

Reading — Telegram

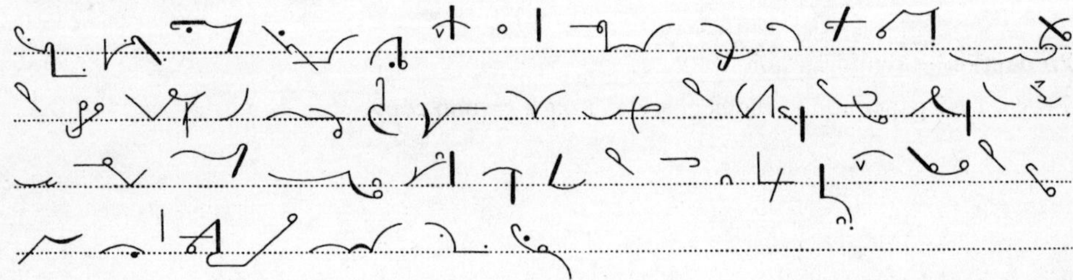

Dictation

FREDERICK TILBURY GRANGE	COMPLETED APPLICATION
PAPER COMPANY LIMITED	FORMS RECEIVED FOR [40]
LEEDS MY DEPARTMENT HAS [10]	APPOINTMENT NEW EXPORT
HAD EXTREMELY URGENT	MANAGER INTERVIEWS
ENQUIRY FROM LARGE	SCHEDULED MIDDLE JANUARY
CORPORATION HANDLING	STOP CAN [50] YOU TAKE
INTERNATIONAL BUSINESS [20]	CHARGE DURING MY
STOP SITUATION REQUIRES	ABSENCE STOP PLEASE
PERSONAL ATTENTION SHALL	RING ME [60] AT COMPANY
MAKE ARRANGEMENTS TRAVEL	HEADQUARTERS IMMEDIATELY
ZURICH [30] EARLY NEXT	ERIC FRASER
MONTH STOP THIRTY	(66 words)

Typing Drill

(a) The situation requires my personal attention.   9

(b) Please ring me at Company Headquarters immediately.   10

(c) I shall make arrangements to be in Zurich early next month.   12

Background Information Exercise — Telegrams

Refer to the latest edition of the *Post Office Guide*, issued annually by the Post Office. Look up 'Telegrams' in the index and type a copy of the information which it gives in regard to:

  (i)   Greetings telegrams;
 (ii)   Telegrams sent by Telex;
(iii)   Prepaid reply.

Production — Telegram

Type the telegram from Eric Fraser, using A5 paper turned sideways (or on a telegram form if you have one). Type in blocked capitals with three spaces between words. Type the initial name and address on a separate line. Take a carbon copy.

Answers

Assignment 1, page 7

Canada: Calgary, Edmonton, Montreal, Quebec, Winnipeg.

USA: Chicago, Detroit, Milwaukee, Minnesota, Philadelphia.

Assignment 2, page 9

Bala: Wales; Balaton: Hungary;
Brienz: Switzerland; Como: Italy;
Garda: Italy; Gruyères: Switzerland;
Nantua: France; Siljan: Sweden;
Windermere: England.

Assignment 3, page 11

disappear, unpleasant, unlicensed, impure, inattentive, disapprove, illegitimate, irrelevant, mistrust.

Assignment 4, page 13

(i)   to stir up trouble deliberately;
(ii)   to make an independent struggle against the majority;
(iii) to make a blunt and forthright statement;
(iv)   to pretend not to see what is happening;
(v)   to make a gesture of peace;
(vi)   to indulge in deception.

Assignment 5, page 15

England: Avon, Cleveland, Cumbria, Humberside, North Yorkshire, West Yorkshire.

Wales: Clwyd, Dyfed, Gwent, Gwynedd, Mid Glamorgan, Powys.

Assignment 6, page 17

(i)   An informal inter-office communication.
(ii)   It has no address for either sender or receiver, no salutation or complimentary close.
(iii) May be signed in full or merely initialled by the sender.
(iv)   Either may be used.

Assignment 7, page 19

(i)   men's, women's;
(ii)   child's; 'its' needs no apostrophe;
(iii) children's;
(iv)   can't, you're;
(v)   no apostrophe needed.

Assignment 9, page 23

(i)   me;   (iii) I;
(ii)   I;   (iv)   me.

Assignment 12, page 29

(i)   list of subjects to be discussed at a meeting;
(ii)   a committee appointed to report upon or carry out one particular piece of work;
(iii) a formal proposal that certain action should be taken;
(iv)   a member who has been elected by vote of the members of the organization in accordance with the Constitution;
(v)   the existing circumstances.

Assignment 15, page 35

(i)   practice;
(ii)   practise;
(iii) practice;
(iv)   practice;
(v)   practise.

Assignment 16, page 37

impossible, unfamiliar, irresponsible, invalid, immodest, disagreement, disreputable, unethical.

Assignment 18, page 41

Ordinary, Urgent, Greetings, De luxe, Overnight, Press, Prepaid replies, Code or cipher, Commonwealth Social (GLT), Letter Telegrams (LT).

Assignment 21, page 47

(i)   Principal;
(ii)   principal;
(iii) principle;
(iv)   principal.

Assignment 22, page 49

credible, creditable, desirable, destructible, enjoyable, indelible, indispensable, infallible, laughable, legible, negligible, possible.

Assignment 26, page 57

insincere, unimportant, unfortunate, disorder, imperfect, independence, uncharitable, indiscretion.

Assignment 30, page 65

BBC: British Broadcasting Corporation;
COD: Cash on delivery;
GC: George Cross;
JP: Justice of the Peace;

MS: Manuscript;
OBE: Order of the British Empire;
RSPCC: Royal Society for the Prevention of Cruelty to Children;
UNESCO: United Nations Educational Scientific and Cultural Organization;
UNO: United Nations Organization;
WHO: World Health Organization.

Assignment 32, page 69

ungrateful, disorganize, improbable, irreligious, untruth, invisible, unseemly, inconsistent, impenetrable.

Assignment 33, page 71

(i) uninhabited;
(ii) depreciating;
(iii) deteriorating;
(iv) infallible;
(v) fragile.

Assignment 35, page 75

(i) who;
(ii) whom;
(iii) whom;
(iv) who.

Assignment 36, page 77

(i) a record of all decisions reached at a meeting;
(ii) a group of members selected to consider specialized topics;
(iii) a motion which has gained the support of the majority of the committee becomes a resolution;
(iv) a person invited to join the committee because of special knowledge or distinction;
(v) the vote which may be cast by the Chairman in order to break the deadlock resulting from a tie in the voting on a motion.

Assignment 37, page 79

irregular, unpractical (impractical — American), impossibility, ungrateful, involuntary, uncivil.

Assignment 38, page 81

Basildon, America, lovely, sum-mer, holi-days, oppor-tunity, arrange-ments, dis-cuss.

Assignment 40, page 85

CIF: Cost, insurance and freight;
COY: Company;
DSO: Distinguished Service Order;
ENC: Enclosure;
IE: That is (*id est*);
INC: Incorporated or inclusive;
MA: Master of Arts;
MP: Member of Parliament;
SAE: Stamped addressed envelope;
SS: Steamship.

Assignment 44, page 93

Austria: Schilling;
Canada: Dollar;
Denmark: Krone;
France: Franc;
Netherlands: Guilder;
Italy: Lira;
Portugal: Escudo;
Spain: Peseta.

Assignment 45, page 95

formulae, memoranda, agendas, sons-in-law, women, courts-martial.

Assignment 46, page 97

informa-tion, anni-versary, wed-ding, scholar-ship, school, recog-nized, univer-sity, dis-tant.

Assignment 48, page 101

Avon: Bristol;
Bedfordshire: Luton;
Cheshire: Crewe;
Dyfed: Lampeter;
Humberside: Bridlington;
South Yorkshire: Doncaster;
Surrey: Leatherhead;
Tyne and Wear: Whitley Bay;
Wiltshire: Salisbury.

Assignment 49, page 103

acreage, argument, careful, committee, comparatively, embarrass, referred, seize.

Assignment 50, page 105

attributable, contemptible, susceptible, penetrable, indelible, perishable, noticeable, impossible, tangible.